T0209679

An Analysis of

Friedrich Nietzsche's

Beyond Good and Evil
Prelude to a Philosophy
of the Future

Don Berry

Published by Macat International Ltd
24:13 Coda Centre, 189 Munster Road, London SW6 6AW.

Distributed exclusively by Routledge
2 Park Square, Milton Park, Abingdon, Oxon OX14 4RN
711 Third Avenue, New York, NY 10017, USA

Routledge is an imprint of the Taylor & Francis Group, an informa business

www.macat.com
info@macat.com

Cataloguing in Publication Data
A catalogue record for this book is available from the British Library.
Library of Congress Cataloguing-in-Publication Data is available upon request.
Cover illustration: Etienne Gilfillan

ISBN 978-1-912303-09-0 (hardback)
ISBN 978-1-912127-75-7 (paperback)
ISBN 978-1-912281-97-8 (e-book)

Notice
The information in this book is designed to orientate readers of the work under analysis,
to elucidate and contextualise its key ideas and themes, and to aid in the development
of critical thinking skills. It is not meant to be used, nor should it be used, as a
substitute for original thinking or in place of original writing or research. References and
notes are provided for informational purposes and their presence does not constitute
endorsement of the information or opinions therein. This book is presented solely for
educational purposes. It is sold on the understanding that the publisher is not engaged
to provide any scholarly advice. The publisher has made every effort to ensure that
this book is accurate and up-to-date, but makes no warranties or representations with
regard to the completeness or reliability of the information it contains. The information
and the opinions provided herein are not guaranteed or warranted to produce particular
results and may not be suitable for students of every ability. The publisher shall not be
liable for any loss, damage or disruption arising from any errors or omissions, or from
the use of this book, including, but not limited to, special, incidental, consequential or
other damages caused, or alleged to have been caused, directly or indirectly, by the
information contained within.

CONTENTS

THE MACAT LIBRARY

The Macat Library is a series of unique academic explorations of seminal works in the humanities and social sciences – books and papers that have had a significant and widely recognised impact on their disciplines. It has been created to serve as much more than just a summary of what lies between the covers of a great book. It illuminates and explores the influences on, ideas of, and impact of that book. Our goal is to offer a learning resource that encourages critical thinking and fosters a better, deeper understanding of important ideas.

Each publication is divided into three Sections: Influences, Ideas, and Impact. Each Section has four Modules. These explore every important facet of the work, and the responses to it.

This Section-Module structure makes a Macat Library book easy to use, but it has another important feature. Because each Macat book is written to the same format, it is possible (and encouraged!) to cross-reference multiple Macat books along the same lines of inquiry or research. This allows the reader to open up interesting interdisciplinary pathways.

To further aid your reading, lists of glossary terms and people mentioned are included at the end of this book (these are indicated by an asterisk [*] throughout) – as well as a list of works cited.

Macat has worked with the University of Cambridge to identify the elements of critical thinking and understand the ways in which six different skills combine to enable effective thinking.
Three allow us to fully understand a problem; three more give us the tools to solve it. Together, these six skills make up the **PACIER** model of critical thinking. They are:

ANALYSIS – understanding how an argument is built
EVALUATION – exploring the strengths and weaknesses of an argument
INTERPRETATION – understanding issues of meaning

CREATIVE THINKING – coming up with new ideas and fresh connections
PROBLEM-SOLVING – producing strong solutions
REASONING – creating strong arguments

To find out more, visit **WWW.MACAT.COM.**

CRITICAL THINKING AND *BEYOND GOOD AND EVIL*

Primary critical thinking skill: CREATIVE THINKING
Secondary critical thinking skill: INTERPRETATION

No philosopher could be a better example of creative thinking in action than Friedrich Nietzsche: a German iconoclast who persistently attacked not only the views of other great philosophers, but also the dominant ideals and assumptions of his contemporary Europe – in culture and the arts, politics, morality, academia, and science.

Creative thinkers are people who redefine issues and topics in novel ways to create new connections, explanations and hypotheses – people, in short, who can turn a topic on its head and present it in an entirely new light. Nietzsche called them "free spirits" – those unwilling to accept the dogmas they find prevalent in society, wanting instead to think and act for themselves. In Beyond Good and Evil, Nietzsche focuses his attention on the underlying assumptions of contemporary life in Germany and Europe more broadly, unleashing a powerful polemical critique of modern values.

His book, which remains one of the most influential works of moral philosophy ever written, is not just an example of creative thinking at work: it is also a passionate argument for its importance. As Nietzsche wrote, "Morality in Europe … is the morality of herd animals." But if one is ready to think differently and stand out from the herd, "other (and especially higher) moralities are … possible."

ABOUT THE AUTHOR OF THE ORIGINAL WORK

Friedrich Nietzsche (1844–1900) was a German philosopher, classical scholar, and student of the history of languages. Instead of following his father and grandfather into the Church, Nietzsche became a professor of philology (the study of the historical development of languages) at the age of just 24. His approach to philosophy combined this historical and classical scholarship with ideas drawn from natural science. He wrote many books, all of which were almost entirely ignored in his lifetime. Nietzsche left academic life in 1879 and suffered a breakdown in 1889 from which he never recovered. He died 11 years later having never seen how influential his writings would become, and his genius was only truly recognized in the twentieth century.

ABOUT THE AUTHOR OF THE ANALYSIS

Dr Don Berry holds a PhD in philosophy from University College London and an honors degree in mathematics from Cambridge. His research focuses on virtue ethics.

ABOUT MACAT

GREAT WORKS FOR CRITICAL THINKING

Macat is focused on making the ideas of the world's great thinkers accessible and comprehensible to everybody, everywhere, in ways that promote the development of enhanced critical thinking skills.

It works with leading academics from the world's top universities to produce new analyses that focus on the ideas and the impact of the most influential works ever written across a wide variety of academic disciplines. Each of the works that sit at the heart of its growing library is an enduring example of great thinking. But by setting them in context – and looking at the influences that shaped their authors, as well as the responses they provoked – Macat encourages readers to look at these classics and game-changers with fresh eyes. Readers learn to think, engage and challenge their ideas, rather than simply accepting them.

'Macat offers an amazing first-of-its-kind tool for interdisciplinary learning and research. Its focus on works that transformed their disciplines and its rigorous approach, drawing on the world's leading experts and educational institutions, opens up a world-class education to anyone.'

Andreas Schleicher
Director for Education and Skills, Organisation for Economic Co-operation and Development

'Macat is taking on some of the major challenges in university education … They have drawn together a strong team of active academics who are producing teaching materials that are novel in the breadth of their approach.'

Prof Lord Broers,
former Vice-Chancellor of the University of Cambridge

'The Macat vision is exceptionally exciting. It focuses upon new modes of learning which analyse and explain seminal texts which have profoundly influenced world thinking and so social and economic development. It promotes the kind of critical thinking which is essential for any society and economy. This is the learning of the future.'

Rt Hon Charles Clarke, former UK Secretary of State for Education

'The Macat analyses provide immediate access to the critical conversation surrounding the books that have shaped their respective discipline, which will make them an invaluable resource to all of those, students and teachers, working in the field.'

Professor William Tronzo, University of California at San Diego

WAYS IN TO THE TEXT

KEY POINTS

- Friedrich Nietzsche (1844–90) was a German philosopher, scholar, and social critic. Although his work was largely overlooked in his lifetime, it went on to have a huge influence on the twentieth century.

- Nietzsche's *Beyond Good and Evil* powerfully criticizes modern values, politics, and culture, and attempts to reimagine morality in light of the decline in religious belief.

- Beautifully written, witty and insightful, its great achievement was to convincingly challenge many of society's most fundamental beliefs.

Who Was Friedrich Nietzsche?

Friedrich Nietzsche was born in 1844, in the small town of Röcken, Saxony, in German Prussia. He lived until 1900, though his intellectual life was effectively ended by a severe mental breakdown in January 1889, only two years after *Beyond Good and Evil: Prelude to a Philosophy of the Future* was written.

Nietzsche was a German philosopher, philologist* (student of the historical development of languages), and classical scholar. His work was mainly concerned with the consequences of secularism* (the view that society should be free of the influence of organised religion) and atheism* (the belief that God does not exist), which had become widespread since the Enlightenment* of the mid-seventeenth and eighteenth centuries. He looked to explore whether absolute moral values could exist in a world without God, and if so how they would differ from existing Christian beliefs. He was also acutely critical of contemporary culture in Germany. Nietzsche's work was underappreciated during his lifetime, but would go on to have a profound influence; not only on philosophy but on many other fields too.

Nietzsche's family was devoutly religious and included many Lutheran* ministers. Between the ages of 14 and 19, Nietzsche himself attended a particularly traditional boarding school, Schulpforta, which had formerly been a monastery. He had been expected to pursue a career in the Church, and after finishing school he read theology and philology at the University of Bonn in 1864. Defying expectations by quickly losing interest in theology, he followed his tutor, Friedrich Wilhelm Ritschl,* to study philology at the University of Leipzig in 1865.

On Ritschl's recommendation, Nietzsche was appointed associate professor of philology at the University of Basel in 1869, when he was only 24 years old. Despite this early success, ultimately his academic career was a disappointment. In 1879 he retired from his position at the university. This was partly due to health concerns, but also an increasing frustration with academia. Nietzsche spent the following decade—during which all of his major works, including *Beyond Good and Evil,* were written—living a solitary, nomadic life, travelling around France, Germany, Switzerland, and Italy in pursuit of better health.

What Does *Beyond Good and Evil* Say?

In a later autobiographical work *Ecce Homo* (1888), Nietzsche describes his 1886 text *Beyond Good and Evil* as a critique of modernity—"including modern science, modern art—even modern politics." Its aim was to encourage us to question contemporary values in light of the decline of religion. Nietzsche hoped this pursuit would lead us to challenge and ultimately renounce Christian morality and pursue spiritually healthier ways of thinking and feeling. Nietzsche's text aims to clear the way for his "philosophers of the future"[1]—powerful, independent thinkers who will determine a new set of values for humanity to live by.

The text is split into nine parts that together undermine many deeply ingrained moral, cultural, and political attitudes that were dominant in nineteenth-century Germany and remain so in our lives today. In the first part, "On the Prejudices of Philosophers," Nietzsche attacks the rationalist* systems of philosophers such as Immanuel Kant,* René Descartes,* and Benedictus Spinoza,* rejecting their dry technical style of philosophizing. In parts 2 and 3, "The Free Spirit" and "The Religious Character," he describes the dominant idea of a virtuous man as influenced by religious values. He later compares this with his own view of a spiritually healthy human being. After an eclectic mix of aphorisms in part 4, spanning many topics, part 5, "On the Natural History of Morals," explores the roots of how we have arrived at our understanding of the concepts of good and evil.

In part 6, "We Scholars," Nietzsche criticizes a prevalent scientific approach to philosophy and presents an alternative vision of how its practitioners should work: *"true philosophers are commanders and legislators:* they say 'That is how it *should* be!'"[2] This section builds on the criticisms of part 1 to powerfully challenge assumptions that were widespread within academia. Its criticisms are enduringly relevant, particularly when we consider the relationship between science and philosophy today. Part 8 is another section of pressing interest to a current reader, in which Nietzsche attacks the prevailing German nationalism, calling instead for citizens to become "good Europeans."[3] Finally, in parts 7 and 9, "Our Virtues" and "What is Noble?", Nietzsche begins to conceive of a new morality that should replace the Judeo-Christian* ideals he has systematically undermined in the earlier parts of the text.

Why Does *Beyond Good and Evil Matter*?

The themes dealt with in this work are clearly relevant to us today, and many of them even more so now than at the time of writing. These include the leveling effects of democracy, the potentially disastrous consequences of blind nationalism, and the attempt to rectify an ongoing decline in the arts.

According to Nietzsche, the values of contemporary Europe are largely Christian in origin. The ideal human being, as conceived through the influence of these values, is compassionate, meek, selfless, humble, chaste, and pious. But Nietzsche was writing at a time when faith was increasingly being lost in both the divine origins of Christian morality and in the Enlightenment project of attempting to rationalize this moral order without recourse to God, as attempted by thinkers such as Kant and Spinoza. Without belief in either God or the Enlightenment project, we are no longer bound to accept the authority of the traditional Christian morality. Nietzsche considers it to be of the greatest importance that we question the value it now holds for us.

In *Beyond Good and Evil,* Nietzsche persistently critiques our received cultural values, and ultimately comes to reject them. He challenges future philosophers to create a new understanding of the virtues and to construct different, more spiritually worthwhile ideals to live by. As the values he attacks are largely those that still define our society today, this is a challenge that no one can afford to ignore.

Beyond Good and Evil is also worth reading for a number of other reasons. Nietzsche is regarded as one of the finest writers of German prose, and even in translation the text has a striking clarity, immediacy, and elegance, surpassing most other writing on moral philosophy. A concise and often scathing style also makes for a highly entertaining read, as Nietzsche attacks and often ridicules many different thinkers and ideologies (particularly in the provocative part 4, "Epigrams and Entr'actes").

The text also contains dozens of allusions to classical literature and philosophy, the investigation of which a diligent reader will find richly rewarding.

Most impressively, *Beyond Good and Evil* presents us with a vision of how to combine the Enlightenment tradition of rational, scientific investigation with the Romanticist* approach of sensitive, learned inquiry into history and culture.

NOTES

1   Friedrich Nietzsche, *Beyond Good and Evil: Prelude to a Philosophy of the Future,* ed. Rolf-Peter Horstmann and Judith Norman, trans. Judith Norman (Cambridge: Cambridge University Press, 2002), 39.

2   Nietzsche, *Beyond Good and Evil*, 106.

3   Nietzsche, *Beyond Good and Evil*, 132.

SECTION 1
INFLUENCES

THE AUTHOR AND THE HISTORICAL CONTEXT

KEY POINTS

- Friedrich Nietzsche's *Beyond Good and Evil* challenges many of the foundational beliefs that our current society maintains.

- Nietzsche came from a highly religious background and grew up in a household of women.

- He was highly critical of many aspects of his contemporary culture—especially the growing nationalism within the German Empire—and these concerns helped to shape the text.

Why Read This Text?

Beyond Good and Evil is a book written by the German philosopher Friedrich Nietzsche in 1886. Nietzsche later described the text as a *"critique of modernity."*[1] It is made up of nine sections, which together offer a sustained criticism of cultural, intellectual, and moral life in the Germany of his day. The book also attempts to attack and refute the ideas and approaches of the author's philosophical predecessors such as Plato,* Descartes* and Kant.*

Perhaps the most important reason for continuing to study the work today is its attack on contemporary Judeo-Christian* moral values, which center on selflessness, charity, piety, and compassion. In "On the Natural History of Morals," the fifth part of *Beyond Good and Evil*, Nietzsche aims to destabilize these ideals and discourage us from taking our inherited moral framework for granted. In a world where morality is no longer supported by religious belief, and many people

> ❝ Nietzsche's life is surely not a success story; on the contrary, it is a rather sad story of misery and failure. It is the story of a man who from the beginning of his adult life, until the sudden and catastrophic end of his productive period, was confronted with embarrassing and humiliating experiences. This is true of his private life as well as of his relations with the intellectual community of his time. ❞
>
> Rolf-Peter Horstmann, *Beyond Good and Evil: Prelude to a Philosophy of the Future*, Introduction

have become skeptical of existing conceptions of "good" and "evil," Nietzsche passionately implores future philosophers to supply us with new values to live by. The text also addresses political themes, advocating the abandonment of petty national differences in pursuit of the development of true greatness.

Author's Life

Nietzsche was born in October 1844, in Prussian Saxony, in the small village of Röcken. He came from a strictly religious Protestant family; not only his father, Carl, but his uncle and both grandfathers were ministers. However, Nietzsche's father died in 1849, and his brother the year after, following which he was raised in a "feminine and pious"[2] household consisting of his mother, a grandmother, two aunts, and his sister, Elizabeth. He found the society of his mother and sister particularly "oppressive and distasteful,"[3] which may go some way to explaining his generally negative attitude to women evident in many parts of *Beyond Good and Evil*.

Nietzsche was expected to follow in the pious family tradition, and between the ages of 14 and 19 attended Schulpforta, a well-known boarding school that had formerly been a Cistercian monastery.

However, when he enrolled at the University of Bonn to read theology and philology* he quickly abandoned theology, and in 1865 transferred to the University of Leipzig with his "favorite teacher,"[4] the classical scholar Friedrich Ritschl,* to continue his study of philology. Nietzsche's work would later include a series of devastating attacks on organized religion—especially Christianity.

After serving briefly as an orderly in the military, in 1869 Nietzsche was appointed associate professor of philology at the University of Basel at the precocious age of 24, thanks in part to a recommendation from Ritschl, who wrote that he had "never had such a talented student."[5] In 1879 Nietzsche withdrew from academia, partly because of increasingly ill health but also because of a growing disdain for scholarly life. *Beyond Good and Evil* was composed during a decade spent traveling alone around various Swiss, Italian, French, and German towns in search of living conditions that would benefit his health and work. This transient period continued until 1889 when he suffered the mental breakdown that would permanently end his intellectual career.

Author's Background

Nietzsche wrote *Beyond Good and Evil* in 1886, 15 years after the unification of the German Empire, which was largely the result of efforts by Otto von Bismarck,* the long-serving Prussian prime minister. Generally speaking, this was a time of increased cultural, political, and intellectual confidence, and belief in science was high. For Nietzsche, however, science was unable to replace Christian values, which it was now necessary to discard since the "Death of God" (this phrase was Nietzsche's way of expressing the declining influence of the Christian religion). Furthermore, Nietzsche saw German culture as degenerate and unoriginal, lacking a "unity of artistic style."[6]

Nietzsche was also "increasingly appalled by the political atmosphere"[7] in Germany, and wrote most of his works in voluntary exile after leaving the University of Basel. Nationalism is vehemently criticized throughout the text, and in response to growing anti-Semitism he writes that "the Jews are without a doubt the strongest, purest, most tenacious race living in Europe today."[8]

Nietzsche contrasts German "morality" with *"realpolitik,"** a politics based on pragmatic considerations of power and military strength rather than majority consent.

NOTES

1   Friedrich Nietzsche, *The Anti-Christ, Ecce Homo, Twilight of the Idols*, trans. Judith Norman (Cambridge: Cambridge University Press, 2005), 135.

2   Frederick Copleston, *A History of Philosophy, Volume 7: 18th and 19th Century German Philosophy* (London: Bloomsbury, 2013), 390.

3   Friedrich Nietzsche, *Beyond Good and Evil: Prelude to a Philosophy of the Future*, introduction, x.

4   Walter Kaufmann, *Nietzsche: Philosopher, Psychologist, Antichrist* (New Jersey: Princeton University Press, 1974), 24.

5   Rüdiger Safranski, *Nietzsche: A Philosophical Biography*, trans. Shelley Frisch (London, Granta Books, 2002), 45.

6   Friedrich Nietzsche, *Untimely Meditations*, ed. Daniel Breazeale, trans. R. J. Hollingdale, (Cambridge: Cambridge University Press, 1997), 5.

7   Friedrich Nietzsche, *On the Genealogy of Morality*, trans. Maudemarie Clark and Alan Swensen (Indianapolis: Hackett, 1998), 9.

8   Friedrich Nietzsche, *Beyond Good and Evil: Prelude to a Philosophy of the Future*, 142.

MODULE 2
ACADEMIC CONTEXT

KEY POINTS

- Philosophers before Nietzsche had typically been concerned with finding timeless and absolute truths through rational* methods.

- At that time this practice had become unsettled by the popular advancement of Darwinian* theory.

- Other philosophers at the time were combining philosophy with psychology and evolutionary theory, but Nietzsche advanced this research by adding history and classical scholarship into the mix.

The Work in its Context

In the early modern* and Enlightenment* periods, moral philosophers tried to identify general moral truths about how we should act, and then justified them with abstract, logical arguments. The Enlightenment can be broadly understood as an attempt to move away from long-held beliefs grounded in religion or tradition. Yet early medieval* thinkers such as Saint Anselm,* Peter Abelard* and Thomas Aquinas* had also produced secular, rational moral arguments alongside their theological works, and their ethical views still exerted an influence on later thinkers. This abstract, logical manner of moral inquiry also has connections to ancient Greek philosophy and especially to Plato* and Socrates.*

This approach was challenged by the defining intellectual achievement of Nietzsche's era: Charles Darwin's* *On the Origin of Species*, published in 1859. Darwin argued that species are not absolute and change over time, and that life descends from a common source

> 66 And perhaps the time is very near when we will realize again and again just *what* actually served as the cornerstone of those sublime and unconditional philosophical edifices that the dogmatists used to build—some piece of folk superstition from time immemorial (like the soul-superstition that still causes trouble as the superstition of the subject of I), some word-play perhaps, a seduction of grammar or an over-eager generalization from facts that are really very local, very personal, very human-all-too-human. 99
>
> Friedrich Nietzsche, *Beyond Good and Evil: Prelude to a Philosophy of the Future*

via a branching pattern. His groundbreaking work emphasized our animal inheritance and our kinship with other species, disputing the Enlightenment idea that humans are separate from nature and therefore able to consider it objectively. This paved the way for naturalistic philosophers such as Nietzsche to combine philosophy with psychology and natural history: "The greatest part of conscious thought must still be attributed to instinctive activity, and this is even the case for philosophical thought."[1]

Overview of the Field

Several important philosophical projects are referred to throughout Nietzsche's *Beyond Good and Evil*. In his seminal work *Meditations on First Philosophy*, Descartes had tried to prove the existence of himself, of God, and of the external world. Finding that he could not doubt his own existence—*cogito ergo sum** (I think, therefore I am)—he built his account of reality from this foundational proposition. Using similar rational methods, eighteenth-century Anglo Irish philosopher George Berkeley* tried to show that all of reality is a mental construct based on sense perception, an idea he advances in works such as *Two Dialogues Between Hylas and Philonous*. In a similar style, Arthur Schopenhauer* proposed in his magnum opus *The World as Will and Representation* that will is the fundamental reality. Lastly, Kant* had attempted to give a justification of Christian morality by deriving it from rules which any rational being would follow.

However, Nietzsche criticizes all of these ideas, regarding Descartes as "superficial," Schopenhauer as "exaggerating a *popular prejudice*,"[2] dismissing Kant's arguments as mere "tartuffery" (showy absurdity),[3] and those of Spinoza,* who attempted a similar project to Kant, as mere "hocus pocus."[4] This failure of Kant and Spinoza—and of others such as David Hume,* Denis Diderot* and Adam Smith*—to justify Christian morality was particularly important for Nietzsche, as "the breakdown of this project provided the historical background against which the predicaments of our own culture can become intelligible."[5]

Another strand of philosophy closer to Nietzsche's own naturalistic position was being developed by a group of thinkers Nietzsche refers to as the "English Psychologists." They tried to explain morality using Darwin's ideas about natural selection,* arguing that the preexisting morality benefited society. Yet, for Nietzsche, these thinkers lacked "the *historical spirit*"[6] and were merely "hypothesizing into the blue."[7] What was needed instead was a more diligent historical inquiry into the origins of morality, and not just the application of evolutionary biology.

Academic Influences

As the "starting point for almost all later German philosophy"[8] Kant was bound to be an influence on Nietzsche. But, by the time he was writing *Beyond Good and Evil,* Nietzsche spoke of him with condescension, writing of his "stiff yet demure tartuffery".[9] Nietzsche's "great teacher Schopenhauer"[10] is also important for understanding his thought, and Nietzsche wrote an essay extolling "*Schopenhauer as*

Educator" as part of his *Untimely Meditations* series. Friedrich Lange's* 1865 book *The History of Materialism and Criticism of Its Present Importance*[11] influenced Nietzsche greatly, and in the late 1860's he wrote "Kant, Schopenhauer and this book by Lange—I do not need anything else."[12]

There were also many other philosophical thinkers who influenced Nietzsche. Ralph Waldo Emerson,* the American essayist, was responsible for "Nietzsche's very first important encounter with philosophy" and was perhaps his "most read and reread author."[13] Plato, whom Nietzsche "refers to more frequently than any other with the exception of Schopenhauer,"[14] was seen as his "true great opponent".[15] The French Moralists, such as La Rochefoucauld,* influenced his pithy, aphoristic writing style. Nietzsche's thinking was also shaped by the many Ancient Greek philosophers he encountered in his career as a philologist, such as Heraclitus* and Democritus.*

Lastly, another central influence was the composer Richard Wagner.* Throughout his career Nietzsche insisted that German culture was in a state of decline, and aimed to encourage its revitalization. The music of Wagner—whom Nietzsche once named "the greatest benefactor" of his life—was initially a source of hope. However, Nietzsche later became disillusioned as the composer turned away from a "healthy sensuality"[16] to become increasingly pious, with later works such as *Parsifal** dealing with explicitly Christian themes.

NOTES

1 Friedrich Nietzsche, *Beyond Good and Evil: Prelude to a Philosophy of the Future,* ed. Rolf-Peter Horstmann and Judith Norman, trans. Judith Norman (Cambridge: Cambridge University Press, 2002), 6–7.

2 Nietzsche, *Beyond Good and Evil,* 18.

3 Nietzsche, *Beyond Good and Evil,* 3.

4 Nietzsche, *Beyond Good and Evil,* 8.

5   Alasdair MacIntyre, *After Virtue* (London: Bloomsbury, 2011), 46–7.

6   Friedrich Nietzsche, *On the Genealogy of Morality*, trans. Maudemarie Clark and Alan Swensen (Indianapolis: Hackett, 1998), 10.

7   Nietzsche, *Genealogy*, 6.

8   Thomas H. Brobjer, *Nietzsche's Philosophical Context* (Chicago: University of Illinois Press, 2008), 36.

9   Nietzsche, *Beyond Good and Evil,* 8.

10   Nietzsche, *Genealogy*, 4.

11   Friedrich Albert Lange, *The History of Materialism and Criticism of Its Present Importance*, trans. Ernest Chester Thomas (Charleston: Nabu Press, 2011).

12   Brobjer, *Nietzsche's Philosophical Context*, 35.

13   Brobjer, *Nietzsche's Philosophical Context*, 22–3.

14   Brobjer, *Nietzsche's Philosophical Context*, 25.

15   Brobjer, *Nietzsche's Philosophical Context*, 28.

16   Nietzsche, *Genealogy*, 69.

THE PROBLEM

KEY POINTS

- The core goal of *Beyond Good and Evil* is to critique the values of Nietzsche's contemporary culture, as a prelude to the creation of new and healthier values.

- The most influential contemporary approaches to moral philosophy were Kant* and Spinoza's* rationalism* and Bentham* and Mill's* utilitarianism.*

- Nietzsche dismissed both types of theory, instead employing a new approach to moral questions that draws from natural history, anthropology, and aesthetics.

Core Question

The main concern of Friedrich Nietzsche's *Beyond Good and Evil: Prelude to a Philosophy of the Future* is to radically readdress the question of what ideals European society should live by. An entirely new range of possibilities had opened up here, due to "the unstoppable decline of faith in the Christian God."[1]

Other moral philosophers since the Enlightenment* such as Hume,* Kant,* Smith,* and Diderot* had not been concerned with this broader cultural problem; they were more interested in justifying existing morality by means of secular reasoning. Yet they had all inherited the content of their moral beliefs "'from their shared Christian past compared with which the divergences between Kant's and Kierkegaard's* Lutheran,* Hume's* Presbyterian* and Diderot's* Jansenist*-influenced Catholic background are relatively unimportant."[2]

> ❝ This book (1886) is in *essence a critique of modernity*, including modern science, modern art—even modern politics—along with indications of an opposite type who is as un-modern as possible, a noble, affirmative type. ❞
>
> Friedrich Nietzsche, *Ecce Homo*

Throughout his body of work Nietzsche strives to bring the presuppositions of this shared Christian morality into question, and in *Beyond Good and Evil* he attempts to connect this key issue to broader cultural concerns. He addresses morality, but only alongside and in relation to science, scholarship, aesthetics, politics, nationalism, and the arts. He viewed all of these individual strands as part of one interconnected question: what overall direction should humanity now follow?

The Participants

For Kant, moral actions derive their worth from the underlying principles on which they are based: "an action from duty has its moral worth *not in the purpose* to be attained by it but in the maxim in accordance with which it is decided upon."[3] His ethics begins by considering humans purely as rational agents and then asking which maxims such agents might adopt. The principles that he derives from this inquiry are his "categorical imperatives,"* universal principles that rational agents necessarily obey because to deny them is to be inconsistent and thus irrational. Kant's theory is deontological,* meaning that duty and moral rules play the foundational role.

For utilitarian thinkers like John Stuart Mill* and Jeremy Bentham,* however, morality is not about being consistent with our rational natures, but only arises because of our capacity to enjoy pleasure and to feel pain. Their ethics centers on the principle of the "greatest happiness of the greatest number," claiming that a morally correct action is always that which maximizes the total happiness of those affected, including animals.

A number of other moral philosophers are discussed in *Beyond Good and Evil*, usually with derision, including rationalists other than Kant such as Spinoza* and Descartes.* Nietzsche also discusses Romantic* thinkers, most notably Schopenhauer.* Lastly, there are the "free thinkers" such as Voltaire,* so called because they believed that truth should be determined through reason rather than through the unquestioning acceptance of tradition. This group he also disparages and contrasts with "free spirits" (such as Nietzsche himself) who are truly breaking free from the limitations of the Christian moral viewpoint.

The Contemporary Debate

Nietzsche was highly critical of both Kantian and utilitarian ethics. He takes it for granted that Kant's arguments are unconvincing, and pokes fun at them rather than providing detailed rebuttals: "The stiff yet demure tartuffery used by the old Kant to lure us along the clandestine, dialectical path that leads the way (or rather: astray) to his 'categorical imperative'—this spectacle provides no small amusement for discriminating spectators like us."[4] For Nietzsche, moral principles are expressions of our individual drives, inclinations, and experiences, so any approach dealing purely in rational argumentation can at most be only a "type of involuntary and unselfconscious memoir."[5] What is needed is a different kind of philosophical inquiry with broader connections to psychology and history.

He is even more dismissive of the advocates of utilitarianism, referring to them as "utilitarian fools."[6] For Nietzsche, to measure moral worth merely in terms of pleasure and pain is to judge things "according to incidental states and trivialities."[7] Such basic subjective feelings are mere "foreground ways of thinking and naïvetés,"[8] and alternative standards such as artistic value give us more suitable metrics for judging actions. He also disputes the neutrality of the utilitarian conception of happiness, showing it to be a culturally specific ideal of "English Happiness": that is, "comfort and fashion (and, at the highest level, for a seat in Parliament)".[9]

NOTES

1   Friedrich Nietzsche, *On the Genealogy of Morality*, trans. Maudemarie Clark and Alan Swensen (Indianapolis: Hackett, 1998).

2   Alasdair MacIntyre, *After Virtue* (London: Bloomsbury, 2011), 62.

3   Immanuel Kant, *Practical Philosophy*, trans. Mary Gregor (Cambridge: Cambridge University Press, 1996), 55.

4   Friedrich Nietzsche, *Beyond Good and Evil: Prelude to a Philosophy of the Future*, ed. Rolf-Peter Horstmann and Judith Norman, trans. Judith Norman (Cambridge: Cambridge University Press, 2002), 8.

5   Nietzsche, *Beyond Good and Evil*, 8.

6   Nietzsche, *Beyond Good and Evil*, 94.

7   Nietzsche, *Beyond Good and Evil*, 116.

8   Nietzsche, *Beyond Good and Evil*, 116.

9   Nietzsche, *Beyond Good and Evil*, 119.

MODULE 4
THE AUTHOR'S CONTRIBUTION

KEY POINTS

- Nietzsche argues that we can no longer view Judeo-Christian morality as absolute and must recognize that we are now free to create our own values.

- Future philosophers should decide new values for society to live by, rather than giving abstract justifications of their inherited morality.

- The suggestion that Judeo-Christian* values be rejected and replaced made *Beyond Good and Evil* unique in its field.

Author's Aims

Friedrich Nietzsche's 1886 work *Beyond Good and Evil: Prelude to a Philosophy of the Future* is "in essence a *critique of modernity*."[1] It sought to destabilize contemporary political and cultural values, and revive what he saw as a degenerate artistic culture.

Due to the decline of religion and the rise of natural science, Nietzsche believed that it was by then impossible for anyone with a strong intellectual conscience to believe in God. The loss of this belief meant that the Christian moral ideals that underpinned contemporary society lacked any absolute foundation. By critiquing these values and attempting to identify their historical sources, Nietzsche aimed to clear a space for his "philosophers of the future"[2] to legislate new ideals for society to strive towards.

Other philosophers had tried to show that a secular justification for Christian morality was available, but Nietzsche considered this a project that was bound to fail. His concerns also went beyond morality, addressing broader contemporary culture. He was particularly

> ❝ The question Nietzsche lays at the feet of his readers, put simply and starkly, is: *What in us wants truth?* He asks repeatedly, and shows how the pursuit of truth takes curious turns. He does not deny truth; rather he challenges dominant assumptions we have about the good of truth and its normative force: *Why not prefer untruth?* ❞
>
> Christa Davis Acampora and Keith Ansell Pearson, *Nietzsche's Beyond Good and Evil*

concerned that the influence of growing democratic and nationalist sensibilities would restrict the development of truly great individuals.

Approach

Nietzsche's attempt to undermine existing values required a different approach to his philosophical predecessors and contemporaries. It was vital to make clear that the Christian interpretation of Good and Evil represented only one of many possibilities for ethical life. This point can only really be made through detailed anthropological study of other cultures and their alternative value systems.

Nietzsche takes the view that moral, political and cultural questions cannot be split up into isolated areas of inquiry. The question of how we should choose to live, both individually and collectively, should encompass "modern science, modern art—even modern politics," and long sections of the book discuss German culture and what he correctly anticipated would become a dangerous rise in nationalism.

For Nietzsche, previous philosophers had not attempted this kind of radical, expansive inquiry and had instead engaged in the "finding of bad reasons for what we believe on instinct."[3] Nietzsche is uninterested in recounting their views, and when he does discuss other philosophers he tends to do so in an acerbic, scornful tone, rather than earnestly addressing their arguments.

Contribution in Context

Nietzsche's naturalistic approach to the study of values relates to another school of thought he later referred to as the "English psychologists."*[4] This group of thinkers, which included Paul Rée* and Herbert Spencer,* had been influenced both by the utilitarians* and by Darwin's* work on natural selection.* In his 1877 book *On the Origins of Moral Sensations*, Rée argued that "moral phenomena can be traced back to natural causes just as much as physical phenomena"[5] and that morality is an adaptation* arising due to its social utility. What was missing from their approach was a sensitivity to cultural context. Like the rationalists,* they assumed that their particular idea of ethics was the only one possible. For Nietzsche, this "lack of historical sense" was the "hereditary defect" of philosophers, and "what is needed now is historical philosophizing, and with it the virtue of modesty."[6]

Nietzsche's achievement was to draw out the consequences of Enlightenment* secularism* and reveal that the traditional foundations of morality had since slipped away. This means that a different kind of inquiry is now necessary—concerned not with abstract truth, but with legislating new ideals for society to live by that will contribute to spiritual growth and the flourishing of culture and the arts. All of this necessitated fundamentally questioning Christian morality. According to Nietzsche, only one philosopher had come close to taking up this perspective: "the issue for me," he later wrote, "was the *value* of morality—and over this I had to struggle almost solely with my great teacher Schopenhauer."[7]

NOTES

1 Friedrich Nietzsche, *The Anti-Christ, Ecce Homo, Twilight of the Idols*, trans. Judith Norman (Cambridge: Cambridge University Press, 2005).

2 Friedrich Nietzsche, *Beyond Good and Evil: Prelude to a Philosophy of the Future,* ed. Rolf-Peter Horstmann and Judith Norman, trans. Judith Norman (Cambridge: Cambridge University Press, 2002), 39.

3   Walter Kaufmann, *Nietzsche: Philosopher, Psychologist, Antichrist* (New Jersey: Princeton University Press, 1974), 103.

4   Friedrich Nietzsche, *On the Genealogy of Morality*, trans. Maudemarie Clark and Alan Swensen (Indianapolis: Hackett, 1998), 9.

5   Paul Rée, *Basic Writings*, ed. and trans. Robin Small (Urbana: University of Illinois Press, 2003), 87.

6   Bernard Williams, *Truth and Truthfulness* (Princeton: Princeton University Press, 2002).

7   Nietzsche, *Genealogy*, 4.

SECTION 2
IDEAS

MAIN IDEAS

KEY POINTS

- In *Beyond Good and Evil*, Nietzsche attacks the culture and politics of his society and begins to describe a new and higher kind of human life lying beyond its boundaries.

- Nietzsche argues that the Judeo-Christian* values held by contemporary Europeans were restricting the development of what he considered the most valuable type of person.

- Nietzsche pursues this theme across nine interrelated but self-contained sections.

Key Themes

In *Beyond Good and Evil*, Friedrich Nietzsche addresses what he saw as the spiritual and cultural decline of Europe in general and Germany in particular. He intended his ideas and writings to counter this decline, as would those of others he hoped would be inspired by his work: his "philosophers of the future."[1] These future thinkers would determine new values for society to live by, and in doing so draw Europe out of its spiritual malaise: "true philosophers are commanders and legislators: they say 'That is how it *should* be!'"[2] Even the value of truth itself would be called into question by this radical new endeavor. Nietzsche suggests the pursuit of truth be second to human flourishing: "We do not consider the falsity of a judgment as itself an objection to a judgment; this is perhaps where our new language will sound the most foreign."[3]

Nietzsche judged that the overall direction of European culture was dictated by the Judeo-Christian morality that predominated at that time, and, to a large extent, still does today. This system centers on

> ❝ Morality in Europe these days is the morality of herd animals—and therefore, as we understand things, it is only one type of human morality beside which, before which, and after which many other (and especially *higher*) moralities are or should be possible. ❞
>
> Friedrich Nietzsche, *Beyond Good and Evil: Prelude to a Philosophy of the Future*

the ideals of selflessness, compassion, humility, chastity, and piety, which were viewed as the most important virtues despite the decline in Christian belief and practice since the Enlightenment.* Also prevalent were democratic and egalitarian values, which saw people as equal and tried to make life as comfortable as possible for everyone. As with the morality of Christianity, Nietzsche regarded these popular beliefs as limitations on mankind's true greatness and believed they hindered the development of what he considered the most valuable type of human being.

What is required, in his view, is twofold: a "typology of morals"[4] documenting the different kinds of morality in existence, and then a ranking to define which of them is most conducive to mankind's proper spiritual development. This is Nietzsche's proposed "revaluation of all values." In order to make this determination in a truly objective spirit, we must set aside our conventional moral beliefs so it can take place "beyond good and evil."

Exploring the Ideas

Once the apparent uniqueness and absoluteness of Christian ethics is convincingly undermined, it becomes possible to compare and contrast the different moral codes that have existed throughout history and in different parts of the world. Nietzsche concludes that all moralities fall into one of two basic types: "a *master morality* and a *slave morality.*"[5] The former is the province of strong, noble, individuals who label themselves as good, in contrast to others who lack those qualities; the latter is the territory of weak, petty, subjugated peoples who first label the aforementioned category of powerful, dominating, and potentially dangerous types as "evil." In parts 7 and 9 of the text—entitled "Our Virtues" and "What is Noble?"—Nietzsche begins to outline a new master morality, based on nobility and the observance of proper distinctions of rank, to rival the dominant Christian slave morality. However, "the title question *What is Noble?* is not as much answered as it is given to the *reader* to ask and explore."[6]

For Nietzsche, our current Christian morality is a herd-morality of individuals who are by nature weak and submissive; through it they exact a kind of spiritual revenge on those who would be their natural masters and superiors. In particular, their egalitarian ideals seek to bring genuinely great and singular individuals down to their level, and "makes them the equal of even people who are teeming with all the qualities and privileges of spirit."[7] Nietzsche's concern then is that this herd-morality, while suitable for certain mediocre types, serves to restrict the development of what he sees as the highest kind of person: strong, creative, cultured individuals such as Goethe,* Mozart,* Stendhal,* Heinrich Heine,* and Beethoven.*

Language and Expression

The text is made up of a preface, a concluding poem, and nine parts loosely dealing with a particular theme, such as giving a "natural history" of our current moral valuations (part 5). These contain some 296 subsections in total, which sometimes run to several pages in length, though many are just a single sentence. In fact, part 4—entitled "Epigrams and Entr'actes"—contains 123 of the subsections, each just one or two sentences in length and offering a short, pithy observation. This aphoristic style enables Nietzsche to switch abruptly from one topic to another.

Nietzsche was keen to elevate himself above the parochial and nationalistic outlook of contemporary Germany and, as one sensitive to nuances of meaning, he often preferred to choose words from other languages if they served his purpose better than German. These languages include French (*petit fait*),[8] Latin (*moribus et artibus*),[9] and Sanskrit (*gangasrotogati*; *kurmagati*).[10] If necessary he would sometimes a coin a new word entirely (*nihiline*).[11] More generally, Nietzsche's prose is vivid, persuasive, and emotively charged. He often opts for expressive and emotive turns of phrase, and his literary style thus contrasts with the dry, technical language characteristic of academic philosophy. Dozens of references to classical literature are also embedded throughout the work.

These stylistic points can be appreciated in light of the aims of the overall project. Nietzsche is not trying to *prove* to us that his particular conclusions are correct. Indeed, he is "suspicious of any thinker who 'has something to prove'."[12] Rather, he aims to open up a critical space of psychological self-exploration that will enable us, his readers, to question our most deeply held values. This will require us to engage emotionally as well as rationally: "The will to overcome an affect is, in the end, itself only the will of another, or several other, affects."[13]

NOTES

1   Friedrich Nietzsche, *Beyond Good and Evil: Prelude to a Philosophy of the Future,* ed. Rolf-Peter Horstmann and Judith Norman, trans. Judith Norman (Cambridge: Cambridge University Press, 2002), 39.

2   Nietzsche, *Beyond Good and Evil*, 106.

3   Nietzsche, *Beyond Good and Evil*, 7.

4   Nietzsche, *Beyond Good and Evil, 75*.

5   Nietzsche, *Beyond Good and Evil*, 153.

6   Christa Davis Acampora and Keith Ansell Pearson, *Nietzsche's Beyond Good and Evil* (London: Continuum, 2011), 25.

7   Nietzsche, *Beyond Good and Evil*, 111.

8   "Little fact." Nietzsche, *Beyond Good and Evil*, 30.

9   "In customs and arts." Nietzsche, *Beyond Good and Evil,* 29.

10 "As the [river] Ganges moves; as the tortoise moves." Nietzsche, *Beyond Good and Evil*, 28.

11 "A neologism coined from 'nihilism'." Nietzsche, *Beyond Good and Evil*, 99.

12 Nietzsche, *Beyond Good and Evil*, 78.

13 Nietzsche, *Beyond Good and Evil*, 65.

MODULE 6
SECONDARY IDEAS

KEY POINTS

- In addition to the principle aim of *Beyond Good and Evil*, Nietzsche addresses a number of striking topics: the shortcomings and dangers of dogmatic philosophy; the nature of the self and how it is constructed from multiple conflicting subconscious drives; and the limiting, and possibly damaging, consequences of narrow-minded German nationalism. He also expresses provocative views about women.

- These ideas have had a significant impact outside of philosophy—on psychology, politics, and culture.

- Perhaps Nietzsche's most important secondary theme is unconscious thought and the nature of the self, which heavily influenced Sigmund Freud* and therefore all of modern psychology.

Other Ideas

In the preface and opening part of *Beyond Good and Evil*, entitled "On the Prejudices of Philosophers," Friedrich Nietzsche takes aim at philosophers such as Kant,* Berkeley,* Spinoza,* and Descartes* who have built up elaborate philosophies from rationalist* principles. Such thinkers—particularly Descartes, whom Nietzsche later labels as "superficial"[1]—are misled by surface features of language, such as "word-play" or a "seduction of grammar."

For Nietzsche, the ultimate causes of our choices are emotional, rather than rational—and this extends to our philosophical beliefs as well. These causes are often not obvious or even visible to us. Nietzsche also gives an account of the self as a combination of competing and

> 66 Suppose that truth is a woman—and why not? Aren't there reasons for suspecting that all philosophers, to the extent that they have been dogmatists, have not really understood women? That the grotesque seriousness of their approach towards the truth and the clumsy advances they have made so far are unsuitable ways of pressing their suit with a woman? What is certain is that she has spurned them—leaving dogmatism of all types standing sad and discouraged. 99
>
> Friedrich Nietzsche, *Beyond Good and Evil: Prelude to a Philosophy of the Future*

conflicting drives. This idea is offered as an alternative to the dominant concept of the self as a simple entity that may be separated from the body: "the soul-superstition that still causes trouble as the superstition of the subject or I."[2]

Nietzsche criticizes women in many places in the book, particularly in part 4 "Epigrams and Entr'actes," and apparently views them as shallow, demure, and secondary to men. His comments would now be regarded as completely unacceptable in a climate that aspires to gender equality; especially *"buona femmina e mala femmina vuol bastone"* (both good and bad women need the stick).[3]

The National Socialist movement later appropriated Nietzsche's writings as a consequence of his sister, Elizabeth Förster-Nietzsche,* taking control of his literary estate in the aftermath of his mental breakdown. While it is clear that the Nazis shared some of his anti-democratic, anti-egalitarian inclinations, popular association of Nietzsche with the movement was deeply unfair. Throughout the text, and particularly in the penultimate part "Peoples and Fatherlands," Nietzsche paints German nationalism in a negative light. He calls instead for the development of "good Europeans,"[4] cultured individuals who are able to transcend the constraints of national pride and move instead towards a unified Europe.

Exploring the Ideas

Immanuel Kant's rationalistic morality is grounded in the notion of a categorical imperative:* a rule that is binding upon all rational agents. Yet for Nietzsche, his arguments are mere sophistry that conceal a personal drive toward the particular ethical system Kant eventually adopts—which happens to be the same one bequeathed to him by his Lutheran* parents. The same is true of the ethics of Spinoza, who casts his arguments in a quasi-mathematical form that is for Nietzsche mere "hocus pocus."[5] Nietzsche also takes aim at the version of idealism* promoted by Berkeley, which views all reality as an immaterial mental construct based on sense experience. Nietzsche points out that our sense organs themselves cannot be seen in this way without contradiction, and so the system falls apart.

Nietzsche also criticizes Descartes' foundationalist epistemology,* as developed in his 1641 work *Meditations on First Philosophy*.[6] In this work, Descartes tries to build up knowledge of the external world beginning from the proposition *cogito ergo sum**—I think, therefore I am—which he takes to be immediate and indubitable. Yet Nietzsche points out that even to understand such a proposition requires us to have "made up my mind what thinking is"—and doing this requires "that I compare my present state with other states that I have seen in myself." Self-evident, immediately apparent knowledge is thus unobtainable, because understanding a proposition always involves understanding a great many other things as well.[7]

This leads to perhaps the most important subsidiary theme in the text: Nietzsche's view of humans as motivated by a multitude of largely unconscious and sometimes amoral drives. This idea would later be absorbed and expanded upon by Sigmund Freud, and through his concept of "the unconscious" would go on to influence psychoanalysis and all of modern psychology.

Overlooked

All of Nietzsche's ideas discussed above influenced academic developments in the twentieth century. However, there remains another significant theme that has been overlooked: moral philosophers have not taken up his call to present a typology (classification) of morality in order of rank. This may be partly because—as Nietzsche himself was so fond of pointing out—philosophers largely lack the historical and scholarly skills necessary for this task. The discipline of anthropology pursues a more neutral description of the distinctive systems of moral valuations of particular cultures, though it stops short of ranking these in order of value. Although some anthropologists have pursued a comparative approach,[8] they do so perhaps more gently than Nietzsche would expect from his commanding and dominating "philosophers of the future."[9]

Another of Nietzsche's overlooked themes is a contribution to an ongoing debate within European politics. Nietzsche "contrasts German nationalism with the sense of belonging to a tradition that exceeds any state's borders."[10] He also frequently points out the cultural and political advantages of an economically unified Europe. Although his views on this matter are of continuing (and, given recent political events, even increasing) relevance, they are often neglected.

NOTES

1 Friedrich Nietzsche, *Beyond Good and Evil: Prelude to a Philosophy of the Future,* ed. Rolf-Peter Horstmann and Judith Norman, trans. Judith Norman (Cambridge: Cambridge University Press, 2002), 81.

2 Nietzsche, *Beyond Good and Evil,* 3.

3 Nietzsche, *Beyond Good and Evil*, 69.

4 Nietzsche, *Beyond Good and Evil*, 132.

5 Nietzsche, *Beyond Good and Evil*, 8.

6 René Descartes, *Meditations on First Philosophy*, ed. and trans. John Cottingham (Cambridge: Cambridge University Press, 1996).

7   Nietzsche, *Beyond Good and Evil*, 17.

8   Jared Diamond, *The World Until Yesterday: What Can We Learn From Traditional Societies?* (New York: Penguin, 2012).

9   Nietzsche, *Beyond Good and Evil*, 39.

10   Christa Davis Acampora and Keith Ansell Pearson, *Nietzsche's Beyond Good and Evil* (London: Continuum, 2011), 2.

MODULE 7
ACHIEVEMENT

KEY POINTS

- In *Beyond Good and Evil*, Nietzsche fulfills his ambition to submit a powerful indictment of modernity.

- Drawing on a vast knowledge of history and classical literature, he is able to show that what were widely regarded as timeless and absolute values are actually highly local and contingent.

- The text is the work of a solitary, socially disengaged individual, who is not yet able to provide us with a viable set of values to live by, in place of those he sets out to undermine.

Assessing the Argument

Friedrich Nietzsche's intention in *Beyond Good and Evil* to critique modernity and our inherited moral values is achieved as powerfully and persuasively as any writer could hope for. As a man who lived on the outskirts of society and led a solitary, nomadic existence, he was uniquely well placed to view the values and ideas of other philosophers, as well as of German culture in general, with detachment.

His cutting criticisms of previous philosophers are often devastating, as he shows many of their solemnly delivered arguments to be based in mere wordplay and sophistry. Anticipating a century of research in psychology, he never tires of insisting that the abstract theorising of even the most highly regarded of his philosophical predecessors was, ultimately, guided and constrained by unconscious instincts of which they were unaware.

> ❝ Virtually everything my generation discussed, tried to think through—one might say, suffered; one might also say, spun out—had long been expressed and exhausted by Nietzsche, who had found definitive formulations; the rest was exegesis. ❞
>
> Gottfried Benn, "*Nietzsche—nach 50 Jahren*"

In destabilizing our inherited morality and sweeping away the rationalizing* arguments of his predecessors, Nietzsche fulfills his greatest ambition for the text: he succeeds in clearing the way for future thinkers to provide new ideals to live by, as a substitute for the Christian framework he attacks. Nietzsche never intended to complete this project within the work itself: in the autobiographical *Ecce Homo* he describes *Beyond Good and Evil* as constituting only the critical, negative, "no-saying" part of the task.[1]

Achievement in Context

Judged on its own, *Beyond Good and Evil* represents a dazzling and brilliant achievement of Nietzsche's intended aims. However, its impact on contemporary culture was not what he had hoped for, largely because its initial circulation was so low: only 114 copies were sold in the first year.[2] Though the history of the work's reception is complicated, particularly considering its harmful association with the Nazi movement, the text has now risen to great prominence. Despite its being so widely read, no philosopher has convincingly taken up the task Nietzsche laid down for future thinkers: to put together a systematic typology of moral systems and instill new values that recognize what human beings need to become spiritually healthy. Although the groundwork was successfully completed, Nietzsche's broader plans have not yet come to fruition.

Nietzsche himself had planned to take on this task in a much longer work, for which he had considered the title "A Re-valuation of All Values." As this title indicates, Nietzsche intended to reassess existing moral valuations: "for once the value of these values must itself be called into question."[3] He aspired to then dictate a new set of values that would allow the greatest examples of humanity to flourish. However, his intellectual life was effectively ended after his mental breakdown of 1889, so this planned constructive work was never written.

Limitations

Some of Nietzsche's criticisms of philosophy in *Beyond Good and Evil* are less relevant now than when the book was written. Nietzsche attacks the grand systemizing of Plato,* Descartes,* and Kant,* arguing that any such system can only be an "unself-conscious memoir" expressing the unacknowledged prejudices and personal characteristics of the writer.[4] Yet this criticism is far less appropriate today—particularly within the analytic* tradition, where thinkers typically focus on narrow, self-contained problems. Philosophers in this tradition also often approach problems through linguistic analysis—and Nietzsche, himself a trained philologist,* often recommended focusing on language.

Another of Nietzsche's criticisms concerns a lack of historical knowledge amongst philosophers. In the nineteenth century, continental* philosophy took up his enthusiasm for philosophy that is grounded in history, and continued to destabilize grand narratives.* Current analytic philosophy is also deeply interested in its own history and that of earlier thinkers, so again Nietzsche's criticism is perhaps less relevant than it once was.

Beyond Good and Evil is also bound to its particular time and culture in its view of women. To give one example of many, Nietzsche writes: 'When a woman has scholarly inclinations, there is usually something wrong with her sexuality."[5] This opinion of female scholarship is obviously outdated, and thinkers such as Elizabeth Anscombe and Martha Nussbaum (amongst a great many others) have clearly shown that women are just as capable of writing great philosophy as men are. Aside from that particular point, his manner of discussing women is notably dated and would be considered deeply offensive from a contemporary perspective.

On the other hand, some of the text is even more relevant now than in its time. For instance, Nietzsche was concerned that democratic and egalitarian ideals served to constrict the development of truly great individuals, who by their nature need to control those to whom they are superior. These individuals also need to suffer intensely in order to become more profound: "suffering makes you noble; it separates."[6] In the advanced democracies of the West today, liberal ideals of universal equality pervade popular discourse even more so than in Nietzsche's time—and the ambition to make life as comfortable as possible is more prevalent than ever.

NOTES

1   Friedrich Nietzsche, *The Anti-Christ, Ecce Homo, Twilight of the Idols*, trans. Judith Norman (Cambridge: Cambridge University Press, 2005), 134.

2   Nietzsche, *Beyond Good and Evil*, introduction, xi.

3   Friedrich Nietzsche, *On the Genealogy of Morality*, trans. Maudemarie Clark and Alan Swensen (Indianapolis: Hackett, 1998), 5.

4   Nietzsche, *Beyond Good and Evil*, 8.

5   Nietzsche, *Beyond Good and Evil*, 69.

6   Nietzsche, *Beyond Good and Evil*, 166.

PLACE IN THE AUTHOR'S WORK

KEY POINTS

- Nietzsche's works are all concerned with a cluster of related themes, including the degeneration of contemporary culture, skepticism about conventional philosophy, natural science, and the detrimental influence of conventional morality and religion.

- The ideas elaborated in *Beyond Good and Evil* are anticipated in earlier works as well as being developed further in later ones.

- *Beyond Good and Evil* is one of Nietzsche's most read works, and is essential to understanding his mature thought.

Positioning

Friedrich Nietzsche's *Beyond Good and Evil* presents perhaps the clearest statement of his mature philosophical views, though most of the ideas it contains appear in earlier publications. In the autobiographical *Ecce Homo*, Nietzsche writes that *Beyond Good and Evil* is "in essence a *critique of modernity*"[1]; this concern with contemporary culture had been a persistent theme since his first book, *The Birth of Tragedy*, in 1872. In the 1878 work *Human, All Too Human*, Nietzsche begins to develop the distinction between master and slave moralities, writing a "*Twofold prehistory of good and evil.*"[2] This is followed by *Daybreak* in 1881, which gives a more thorough appraisal of conventional morality, especially criticizing the idea that "moral" and "selfless" are synonymous with respect to actions.

Nietzsche's 1882 work *The Gay Science* discusses the declining influence of religion upon culture and society, encapsulated in

> ❝ *Beyond Good and Evil* is often considered to be one of Friedrich Nietzsche's greatest books. Though it is by no means clear what criteria this assessment is based on, it is easy to understand how it comes about. It seems to be an expression of the feeling that in this book Nietzsche gives the most comprehensible and detached account of the major themes that concerned him throughout his life. ❞
>
> Rolf-Peter Horstmann, *Beyond Good and Evil: Prelude to a Philosophy of the Future*, Introduction

Nietzsche's famous statement that "God is dead."[3] It also attacks dogmatic, rationalist* philosophy, and Kant* in particular. Between this book and *Beyond Good and Evil*, Nietzsche composed the four parts of *Thus Spoke Zarathustra* (1883–85)—perhaps the book Nietzsche himself valued most highly. In a letter to a friend, Nietzsche wrote of *Beyond Good and Evil* that it "says the same things as my Zarathustra, only differently, very differently"[4]—though in fact the themes often diverge significantly.

On the inside cover of Nietzsche's 1887 work *On the Genealogy of Morality* were the words "Appended to the recently published *Beyond Good and Evil* as a supplement and clarification."[5] In *Genealogy*, Nietzsche offers a historical narrative detailing the origins and development of three aspects of the moral outlook criticized in *Beyond Good and Evil*: our conceptions of right and wrong; our moral consciences; and the "ascetic ideal" wherein the highest human life is seen as one characterized by "poverty, humility, chastity"[6] and self-denial. The ideas of *Beyond Good and Evil* are developed further in later works. *Twilight of the Idols* (1888) continues to argue that the validity of our moral ideals depends essentially on the now-discarded Christian religion. And *The Antichrist* (1888) constitutes an aggressive attack on the Christian religion as a whole, particularly as interpreted by Saint Paul, whom Nietzsche claims has "distorted Christ's real significance."[7]

Integration

Nietzsche's short but productive writing career—beginning with *The Birth of Tragedy* in 1872 and ending with the succession of books written in 1888 before his collapse in January 1889—saw him progress through a number of intellectual stages, and his answers to fundamental questions changed radically in the process. For instance, in *The Birth of Tragedy*, Nietzsche regards the development of the arts as "the highest task"[8] for humanity, whereas by the time he writes *Human, All Too Human* in 1878 it is natural science and the pursuit of truth that take precedence. Moving forward to 1886, in *Beyond Good and Evil* the limitations of science are explored and the value of truth for its own sake is put into question: "The question is how far the judgment promotes and preserves life, how well it preserves, and perhaps even cultivates, the type."[9] Yet by *The Anti-Christ* (1888) truth again appears as a central good, and in *Ecce Homo* Nietzsche views the question of "How much truth can a spirit *tolerate*" as "the real measure of value."[10]

Despite these developments in his thought, a unity emerges in the themes Nietzsche chooses to consider and the way they relate to each other. Throughout his body of work he is concerned with addressing the same cluster of problems: the consequences of declining religious belief—especially with regards to supposedly absolute moral valuations; the decline of contemporary culture more generally, and how best to revive it; and the nature and possibility of objective truth in the sciences and within moral philosophy. Each of these themes receives extended treatment in *Beyond Good and Evil*.

Significance

The route through which Nietzsche gained his reputation as a great thinker is complex. Though his work was largely ignored during his

active lifetime, it would later come to dominate the continental*
philosophical traditions of the twentieth century. Within analytic*
philosophy his initial reception was more frosty, though since the event of
Walter Kaufmann's 1950 book *Nietzsche: Philosopher, Psychologist,
Antichrist*—the "major event of twentieth-century Nietzsche scholarship
in the United States"[11]—practitioners within this tradition have also
begun to take a more serious interest in his work.

As one of his most widely read books, *Beyond Good and Evil* has
contributed to Nietzsche's acceptance into the Western canon of
great philosophers. Written at the peak of his intellectual powers, it
gives perhaps the clearest statement of his views on many of the
recurrent topics of his work, particularly morality. It also elaborates
on his doctrine of perspectivism,* acknowledging the extent to
which our personal context colors our beliefs about the world and
therefore casting doubt on the existence of any absolute or objective
truth. This doctrine Nietzsche describes as "the fundamental
condition of all life."[12]

Though the later work *On the Genealogy of Morality* is more
systematic and addresses morality in more detail, *Beyond Good and Evil*
contains a broader range of themes, canvassing "the whole range of
Nietzsche's interests."[13] Its direct and aphoristic style makes it a
suitable entry point to Nietzsche's thought.

NOTES

1   Friedrich Nietzsche, *The Anti-Christ, Ecce Homo, Twilight of the Idols*, trans.
    Judith Norman (Cambridge: Cambridge University Press, 2005), 135.

2   Friedrich Nietzsche, *Human, All Too Human*, trans. R. J. Hollingdale
    (Cambridge: Cambridge University Press, 1996), 36.

3   Friedrich Nietzsche, *The Gay Science*, ed. Bernard Williams, trans. Josefine
    Nauckhoff (Cambridge; Cambridge University Press, 2001), 120.

4   Quoted in Christa Davis Acampora and Keith Ansell Pearson, *Nietzsche's
    Beyond Good and Evil* (London: Continuum, 2011), 5.

5   Friedrich Nietzsche, *On the Genealogy of Morality*, trans. Maudemarie Clark
    and Alan Swensen (Indianapolis: Hackett, 1998), ɪɪ.

6   Nietzsche, *Genealogy*, 76.

7   Nietzsche, *The Anti-Christ*, introduction, xxɪɪ.

8   Friedrich Nietzsche, *The Birth of Tragedy*, ed. Raymond Geuss and Ronald
    Speirs, trans. Ronald Speirs, (Cambridge: Cambridge University Press,
    1999), 14.

9   Friedrich Nietzsche, *Beyond Good and Evil: Prelude to a Philosophy of the
    Future,* ed. Rolf-Peter Horstmann and Judith Norman, trans. Judith Norman
    (Cambridge: Cambridge University Press, 2002), 7.

10 Nietzsche, *Ecce Homo*, 72.

11 Nietzsche, *Genealogy*, xɪ.

12 Nietzsche, *Beyond Good and Evil*, 4.

13 Nietzsche, *Beyond Good and Evil*, vɪɪɪ.

SECTION 3
IMPACT

THE FIRST RESPONSES

KEY POINTS

- The most influential early review of *Beyond Good and Evil* argued that its attack on conventional morality was a danger to society.

- Nietzsche was largely indifferent to his critics' remarks, and felt his ideas had been deeply misunderstood.

- His work later rose to fame only under the influence of his sister, who wrongly associated it with the German National Socialist* regime.

Criticism

Friedrich Nietzsche's relationship with his critics was always problematic. His first book *On the Birth of Tragedy*, published in 1872, attracted the critical attention of the classicist Ulrich von Wilamowitz-Möllendorff,* who wrote aggressive diatribes against both Nietzsche and his supporter Erwin Rohde.* For Möllendorff, Nietzsche's whimsical speculations were a danger to serious scholarship. He was "harshly critical" of the work, and "dismissive of Nietzsche's whole project."[1] Responses were issued by both Rohde and Richard Wagner,* but the final straw came when Nietzsche's mentor Ritschl* sided with Möllendorff. Though these reviews were amongst Möllendorff's first publications, he went on to be the most influential classical scholar of his era, and the conflict left Nietzsche's reputation as a promising young philologist in tatters. This strongly affected sales of his books, and so *Beyond Good and Evil: Prelude to a Philosophy of the Future* initially sold very few copies.

> ❝ In a review for the Swiss journal *Der Bund*, Josef
> Victor Widmann described [*Beyond Good and Evil*] as
> Nietzsche's 'dangerous book' (*gefährliches Buch*), pointing
> out that the dynamite used in the construction of the
> *Gotthard-bahn*, the railway line that traverses the Swiss
> Alps, always bore a black warning-flag to alert people
> to its danger—and that Nietzsche's book deserved a
> similar warning. ❞
>
> Michael Allen Gillespie and Keegan F. Callanan, *A Companion to Friedrich
> Nietzsche*

Despite the disappointing scale of its reception, it is possible to gauge some of the contemporary reaction to the text. Joseph Viktor Widmann,* the editor of the Swiss daily newspaper *Der Bund*, published a review of *Beyond Good and Evil* entitled "Nietzsche's Dangerous Book,"[2] in which he suggested that Nietzsche was trying to "do away with all decent feelings,"[3] and sought to warn others against what he regarded as the potentially dangerous consequences of Nietzsche's attack on conventional morality. Some reactions to the work were more positive, particularly outside of Nietzsche's native Germany. Indeed, Georg Brandes,* an influential Danish critic and scholar, regarded Nietzsche as a "genius," and delivered a series of lectures on his philosophy at the University of Copenhagen in 1888.

Responses

Perhaps surprisingly, Nietzsche was "delighted"[4] by Widmann's review, both because it sparked more interest in his work and increased sales, and also because it used the metaphor of dynamite to express the explosive power of his ideas. He would later apply this to himself in the autobiographical *Ecce Homo*: "I am not a human being. I am dynamite."[5] There was, however, little opportunity for him to form an active reciprocal relationship with his critics, or for the influence of reviews to be felt in his work. After retiring from the University of Basel for health reasons in 1879, Nietzsche spent the following decade largely in isolation from academic life, and his permanent mental breakdown took place just 18 months after *Beyond Good and Evil*'s publication.

In another section of *Ecce Homo*, provocatively entitled "Why I Write Such Good Books," Nietzsche is scornful of his critics, and responds briefly to unfair charges of idealism* and Darwinism* only "with all the carelessness it warrants."[6] Claiming that it is inevitable that such complex ideas would be misunderstood by unworthy readers, and that "nobody can get more out of things—including books—than they already know,"[7] he asks that we "forgive my complete lack of curiosity about reviews of my books."[8]

Conflict and Consensus

Although Nietzsche had hopes for his growing readership outside of Germany, "in Vienna, in St Petersburg, in Stockholm, in Copenhagen, in Paris and New York,"[9] it would be many years before his work would get the attention it deserved and a consensus view of *Beyond Good and Evil* as one of his "greatest books"[10] would be established. When Nietzsche's name was eventually rescued from "the absurd silence under which it lies buried"[11] it was under the ugliest circumstances imaginable. His sister Elizabeth Förster-Nietzsche* popularized his work by associating it with the German National Socialist party, despite Nietzsche's persistent attacks on both anti-Semitism and German nationalism. This link with Nazi politicians and intellectuals muddied Nietzsche's reputation as a philosopher, and led to attacks by liberal thinkers in the analytic* tradition, notably Bertrand Russell*: "I dislike Nietzsche because he likes the contemplation of pain, because he erects conceit into a duty, because the men whom he most admires are conquerors, whose glory is cleverness in causing men to die."[12]

Nietzsche was not really taken seriously within anglophone philosophy before the landmark publication of Walter Kaufmann's* *Nietzsche: Philosopher, Psychologist, Antichrist* in 1950.[13] Since then Nietzsche's work has received thorough scholarly analysis, which has shown his ideas to be of great relevance to contemporary philosophical concerns. A consensus has emerged that *Beyond Good and Evil* has contributed substantially to cultural criticism as well as moral philosophy.

NOTES

1   Friedrich Nietzsche, *The Birth of Tragedy*, ed. Raymond Geuss and Ronald Speirs, trans. Ronald Speirs (Cambridge: Cambridge University Press, 1999), introduction, xxviii.

2   Joseph Viktor Widmann, "Nietzsche's Dangerous Book," *New Nietzsche Studies* 4 (2000): 195–200.

3   Friedrich Nietzsche, *The Anti-Christ, Ecce Homo, Twilight of the Idols*, trans. Judith Norman (Cambridge: Cambridge University Press, 2005), 101.

4   Michael Allen Gillespie and Keegan F. Callanan, "On the Genealogy of Morals," in *A Companion to Friedrich Nietzsche*, ed. Paul Bishop (New York: Camden House, 2012), 251.

5   Nietzsche, *Ecce Homo,* 142–3.

6   Nietzsche, *Ecce Homo*, 100.

7   Nietzsche, *Ecce Homo*, 101.

8   Nietzsche, *Ecce Homo*, 101.

9   Friedrich Nietzsche, *On the Genealogy of Morality*, trans. Maudemarie Clark and Alan Swensen (Indianapolis: Hackett, 1998), 102.

10 Friedrich Nietzsche, *Beyond Good and Evil: Prelude to a Philosophy of the Future,* ed. Rolf-Peter Horstmann and Judith Norman, trans. Judith Norman (Cambridge: Cambridge University Press, 2002), introduction, vii.

11 Nietzsche, *Ecce Homo,* 143.

12 Bertrand Russell, *History of Western Philosophy* (New York: Routledge, 1996), 697.

13 Nietzsche, *Genealogy*, introduction xi.

MODULE 10
THE EVOLVING DEBATE

KEY POINTS

- Nietzsche's books have inspired and influenced all the central thinkers in continental* philosophy.

- His work has influenced schools of thought as diverse as Marxism* and feminism,* and has acted as a direct stimulus to existentialism,* psychoanalysis,* and postmodernism.*

- His writings have exerted a profound impact on many areas of intellectual life in the twentieth century.

Uses and Problems

Friedrich Nietzsche has been a central influence on many of the most dominant intellectual figures of the twentieth century. Those influenced by Nietzsche include the psychologist Sigmund Freud,* who developed his ideas about hidden, subconscious motivations being the true efficient causes of our actions; the sociologist and cultural critic Theodor Adorno,* who also delivered acerbic polemics against his contemporary culture; the playwright George Bernard Shaw,* whose play *Man and Superman* was inspired by Nietzsche's concept of the Übermensch,* and the novelist James Joyce,* who explored Nietzsche's doctrine of perspectivism* in his influential modernist novel *Ulysses*.[1]

Perhaps the intellectual tradition that Nietzsche has influenced most is continental philosophy, whose practitioners often resemble Nietzsche's "philosophers of the future."[2] They "question the metaphysical* *'belief in oppositions of value'*,"[3] and discuss how our individual experiences can affect the categories we bring to bear when

> ❝ Nietzsche, more than any other philosopher of the past hundred years, represents a major historical event. His ideas are of concern not only to the members of one nation or community, nor alone to philosophers, but to men everywhere, and they have had repercussions in recent history and literature as well as in psychology and religious thought. ❞
>
> Walter Kaufmann, *Nietzsche: Philosopher, Psychologist, Antichrist*

classifying reality. These are both central themes of postmodernism. They are also interested in "declaring war on the metaphysical neglect of the senses,"[4] which is central to phenomenology.* Nietzsche's ideas have given direction to the thought of central continental thinkers, including Martin Heidegger* and Gilles Deleuze,* each of whom has produced book-length studies of his philosophy. Michel Foucault* was especially influenced by Nietzsche's historical approach and when interviewed in 1982 said, "Nietzsche was a revelation to me."[5]

Schools of Thought

Though existentialism* is largely a twentieth-century movement and centers on the philosophy of Jean-Paul Sartre,* it was anticipated and inspired by Nietzsche and Søren Kierkegaard.* Like Nietzsche, existentialists criticize previous philosophy as being too abstract and detached from lived human experience. They too take the radical moral freedom of the human subject—particularly once free of religious belief—as the starting point for philosophical reflection.

Psychoanalysis is both a psychological theory and a practical school of therapy, whose founder and chief theorist Sigmund Freud wrote of Nietzsche that "he had a more penetrating knowledge of himself than any man who ever lived or was likely to live."[6] Psychoanalysts believe that primitive, unconscious drives are the true motivating causes of our behavior rather than any conscious reasoning process, an idea clearly anticipated by Nietzsche in the text. He describes philosophical systems as a "type of involuntary and un-self-conscious memoir"[7] on the part of their authors, and writes that "most of a philosopher's conscious thought is secretly directed and forced into determinate channels by the instincts."[8]

Though postmodernism is a broader cultural movement that extends outside of philosophy, it is strongly associated with the Nietzschean themes of the problematic nature of objective truth, as well as the fundamental importance of power dynamics in determining the outcome of historical events. Its practitioners also tend to uphold Nietzsche's skepticism of "the belief in opposition of values."

In Current Scholarship

Works of Nietzsche's such as *Beyond Good and Evil: Prelude to a Philosophy of the Future* still exert a dominant influence over continental philosophers today, and Gilles Deleuze has claimed it is "clear" that "modern philosophy has largely lived off Nietzsche."[9] Although he is widely read within analytic philosophy, few thinkers in this field have attempted to follow his example directly. Serious Nietzsche scholarship still flourishes in this tradition, however, and there is now a large number of professional Nietzsche scholars, many of who have achieved fame from their work in this area alone. These include Maudemarie Clarke,* Christopher Janaway,* Christa Davis Acampora, John Richardson and Brian Leiter.* Dedicated journals such as *The Journal of Nietzsche Studies* and *New Nietzsche Studies* have also appeared.

A small number of anglophone philosophers have attempted to follow Nietzsche more directly. The philosopher Alasdair MacIntyre* also gives a critique of contemporary values from a historical perspective, publishing a compilation of papers under the title *Against the Self-Images of the Age* (1971). MacIntyre also dismisses Enlightenment attempts to provide a secular rational* justification for morality as unworkable, and regards Nietzsche as a centrally important figure because of his "relentlessly serious pursuit"[10] of this problem. However, for MacIntyre, Nietzsche was limited by his individualist outlook, and did not realise that human flourishing is to a large extent a matter of the quality of the relationships we enjoy with others. The influential moral philosopher Bernard Williams's* 2002 book *Truth and Truthfulness* also combines philosophy with history and psychology, and Williams comments that "the problems that concern this book were discovered, effectively, by Nietzsche."[11]

NOTES

1   Joseph Valente, "Beyond Truth and Freedom: The New Faith of Joyce and Nietzsche," *James Joyce Quarterly* 25, no. 1 (1987): 87–103.

2   Friedrich Nietzsche, *Beyond Good and Evil: Prelude to a Philosophy of the Future,* ed. Rolf-Peter Horstmann and Judith Norman, trans. Judith Norman (Cambridge: Cambridge University Press, 2002), 39.

3   Martine Prange, "Beyond Good and Evil," in *A Companion to Friedrich Nietzsche: Life and Works,* ed. Paul Bishop (New York: Camden House, 2012), 236.

4   Prange, "Beyond Good and Evil," in *A Companion to Friedrich Nietzsche*, 236.

5   Michel Foucault, "Truth, Power, Self: An Interview with Michel Foucault" in *Technologies of the Self,* ed. Luther H. Martin et al. (London: Tavistock, 1988), 9–15.

6   Ernest Jones, *The Life and Work of Sigmund Freud*, vol. II (New York: Basic Books, 1953), 344.

7   Nietzsche, *Beyond Good and Evil,* 8.

8   Nietzsche, *Beyond Good and Evil,* 7.

9   Gilles Deleuze, *Nietzsche and Philosophy*, trans. Hugh Tomlinson (London: Athlone, 1983).

10 Alasdair MacIntyre, *After Virtue* (London: Bloomsbury, 2011), 133.

11 Bernard Williams, *Truth and Truthfulness* (Princeton: Princeton University Press, 2002) 12–13.

IMPACT AND INFLUENCE TODAY

KEY POINTS

- *Beyond Good and Evil* is still widely read by philosophers and is commonly included in undergraduate philosophy courses.

- It throws down a challenge to contemporary values, and to contemporary philosophy in particular, that is largely unanswered.

- Critics have attacked Nietzsche's historicism,* psychologism,* and apparent immoralism.

Position

As a powerful critique of many aspects of modernity, Friedrich Nietzsche's *Beyond Good and Evil* is widely studied today and often included as reading material for contemporary courses in both moral and nineteenth-century philosophy. Within the continental* tradition it still serves to inspire the work of key thinkers. One example of the many important contemporary continental philosophers who have been greatly influenced is Peter Sloterdijk,* who follows Nietzsche's declaration that a philosopher must not only give expression to conventional values but also criticize and change them to better serve humanity's true development. This is a task that requires a certain detachment from contemporary society: "It is no accident that the great representatives of critique—the French moralists, the *Encyclopédists*,* the socialists, and especially Heine,* Marx,* Nietzsche, and Freud*—remain outsiders to the scholarly domain."[1]

Though Nietzsche is also widely read within analytic* university departments, and most philosophers in this tradition are familiar with

> ❝Nietzsche's works may still be captivating because they confront a concern that is not restricted to modern times. They address our uncomfortable feeling that our awareness of ourselves and of the world depends on conceptions that we ultimately do not understand.❞
>
> Rolf-Peter Horstmann, *Beyond Good and Evil: Prelude to a Philosophy of the Future*, Introduction

his central ideas, it is also true that "so many contemporary moral philosophers, particularly of the Anglo-American analytic school, ignore Nietzsche's attack on morality and just go on as if this extraordinary event in the history of thought had never occurred"[2]— often preferring instead to continue with the Enlightenment* project of justifying morality that Nietzsche so convincingly challenged. Though his ideas are taken to be of current intellectual value, rather than merely antiquarian interest, students are not encouraged to imitate the *ad hominem** (personal attack) argumentative style exhibited in the text, and are instead directed toward the "no-nonsense virtues of analytic philosophy" [3]—that is: clarity, logical rigor, and the provision of detailed, detached arguments.

Interaction

Within contemporary moral philosophy in the analytic tradition, Nietzsche's views challenge established research methods in two important ways. First, he argues that moral philosophy should have a closer connection with psychology. The starting point for reflection in analytic moral philosophy today tends to be a set of intuitive and often only partially articulated judgments that are then brought to bear on specific concrete cases, such as Philippa Foot's* trolley problem.* Theorists then aim to systemize and rationalize* these judgments. There is little focus on how the judgments originated in the first place.

For Nietzsche, we should not rely on such intuition unquestioningly, but must always ask "*how* did it emerge there?" and then "*what* is really impelling me to listen to it?"[4]

Second, Nietzsche challenges the assumption that our Judeo-Christian* morality is absolutely binding. This morality says, "I am morality itself and nothing else is moral!"[5] Within contemporary analytic moral philosophy, the belief that selflessness is a virtue is taken for granted. In an important introduction to moral philosophy, the influential philosopher Bernard Williams* writes of selfish or egoist desires that "the contrast between these considerations and the ethical is a platitude,"[6] and this attitude is shared by other practitioners today. Yet Nietzsche argued that alternative ethical frameworks were available, and ultimately concluded that Christian morality stands in the way of human advancement. In part 5, "On the Natural History of Morals," Nietzsche outlines some other possibilities for ethical life outside of this morality of compassion and self-sacrifice—for example the Greco-Roman master morality that revered strength, honor, and bravery.

The Continuing Debate

In contrast to Nietzsche's approach, analytic philosophy has always had an anti-psychologistic focus. Gottlob Frege,* a German logician and key founder of the movement, implores us: "Never let us take the description of the origin of an idea for a definition, or an account of the mental and psychological conditions on which we become conscious of a proposition for a proof of it."[7] From this perspective, in which the truth of any philosophical doctrine is logically independent from the cause of a philosopher adopting it, Nietzsche's emphasis on psychological analysis is misguided and *ad hominem*. Another typical response is to attack Nietzsche's inherent historicism. Writing about MacIntyre's* *After Virtue*, William K. Frankena,* an American moral philosopher, objected that "I can, if I have the right conceptual equipment, understand *what* the view is without seeing it as the result of a historical development; and, so far as I can see, I can also assess its status as true or false or rational to believe without seeing it as such an outcome."[8]

In an article entitled "Nietzsche's Immoralism," Philippa Foot claims that "Nietzsche thought he could discredit morality,"[9] and argues that he is mistaken in this regard. However, Nietzsche is not opposed to morality as such: indeed, he hopes that his philosophers of the future will construct a new morality more in line with humanity's true goals. Nietzsche is merely opposed to a specifically Judeo-Christian interpretation of morality. In challenging the foundations of this morality he is not committed to an outright rejection of compassionate or selfless actions, and indeed writes: "It goes without saying that I do not deny—unless I am a fool—that many actions called immoral ought to be avoided and resisted, or that many called moral ought to be done and encouraged."[10] Nietzsche simply wished to encourage the fundamental questioning of *why* we prioritize some values above others.

NOTES

1   Peter Sloterdijk, *Critique of Cynical Reason*, trans. Michael Eldred (Minnesota: University of Minnesota Press, 1988), 18.

2   Philippa Foot, "Nietzsche's Immoralism," in *Nietzsche, Genealogy, Morality*, ed. Richard Schacht (Berkeley: University of California Press, 1994), 49.

3   Christopher Janaway, *Beyond Selflessness: Reading Nietzsche's Genealogy* (Oxford: Oxford University Press, 2007), vi.

4   Friedrich Nietzsche, *The Gay Science,* ed. Bernard Williams, trans. Josefine Nauckhoff (Cambridge: Cambridge University Press, 2001), 187.

5   Friedrich Nietzsche, *Beyond Good and Evil: Prelude to a Philosophy of the Future,* ed. Rolf-Peter Horstmann and Judith Norman, trans. Judith Norman (Cambridge: Cambridge University Press, 2002), 90.

6   Bernard Williams, *Ethics and the Limits of Philosophy* (Abingdon: Routledge, 2011), 13.

7 Gottlob Frege, *The Foundations of Arithmetic*, trans. J. L. Austin (Oxford: Basil Blackwell, 1980), vi.

8 William K. Frankena, "Review: MacIntyre and Modern Morality," *Ethics* 93, no. 3 (1983): 579–87.

9 Philippa Foot, "Nietzsche's Immoralism," 49.

10 Friedrich Nietzsche, *Daybreak*, ed. Maudemarie Clark and Brian Leiter, trans. R. J. Hollingdale (Cambridge: Cambridge University Press, 1997), 103.

WHERE NEXT?

KEY POINTS

- *Beyond Good and Evil* will continue to influence moral philosophy for many years to come.

- The wealth of ideas it contains has the potential to provide a stimulus to many current schools of philosophical thought, such as naturalism* and Aristotelianism.

- Entertaining, provocative, and exceptionally well written, *Beyond Good and Evil* provides a clear statement of Nietzsche's mature views, and serves as an excellent introduction to his philosophy.

Potential

Beyond Good and Evil: Prelude to a Philosophy of the Future is, with good reason, "often considered to be one of Friedrich Nietzsche's greatest books."[1] Written near the end of his productive life, it contains his most accomplished and complete thoughts on many of the topics he engaged most intimately with, particularly morality and the nature of philosophy. Many themes dealt with in earlier works are developed further, as Nietzsche begins to describe a spiritually superior form of human life that lies outside the existing moralized categories of "good" and "evil," and draws up new tables of the virtues that such human beings would need. As interest in Nietzsche's work looks set to increase, the place of *Beyond Good and Evil* as a central text in the canon of moral philosophy seems assured.

Another reason why the book will continue to attract interest is that it constitutes an attack on modernity. Yet many aspects of Nietzsche's contemporary Germany that he found problematic—the

> **❝** What then the conjunction of philosophical and historical argument reveals is that *either* one must follow through the aspirations and the collapse of the different versions of the Enlightenment project until there remains only the Nietzschean diagnosis and the Nietzschean problematic *or* one must hold that the Enlightenment project was not only mistaken, but should never have been commenced in the first place. There is no third alternative ... **❞**
>
> Alasdair MacIntyre, *After Virtue*

detached and abstract focus of academic philosophy, the increasing cultural authority of empirical science, the decline of the arts, the influence of democratic thinking, and the rise in nationalist fervor— are equally applicable to the twenty-first-century world today. Given that there has not yet been a convincing response to his challenging of Western society's most cherished ideals, Nietzsche's masterpiece will be of continuing relevance to future generations.

Future Directions

There are many emerging contemporary schools of philosophical thought that could benefit from Nietzsche's influence. Of these future prospects, perhaps the most important concerns the resurgence of Aristotelian virtue ethics* during the last half-century.

In an influential 1958 article entitled "Modern Moral Philosophy," Elizabeth Anscombe* argues (with Nietzsche) that our inherited moral framework is based on "concepts of obligation, and duty" that are "survivals, from an earlier conception of ethics" that itself requires belief in moral laws preordained by God—and which are "only harmful without it."[2] Instead she advocates an Aristotelian ethics approach grounded in more realistic moral psychology. Alasdair

MacIntyre's landmark 1981 publication *After Virtue* draws much the same conclusions and has also been influential in popularizing Aristotelianism as a third alternative after consequentialism* and Kantian* deontology*.

For MacIntyre, Nietzsche's arguments are successful in showing that our current morality cannot be justified through abstract reason alone. However, the need for such a project arose only as a consequence of rejecting the much older tradition of moral thought and practice embodied in Aristotle's* writings. Moreover, Nietzsche's arguments against previous philosophers—which attack the abstract, theoretical nature of their thought—are less relevant when directed against Aristotle's more pragmatic approach. If MacIntyre is correct in his assertions, it is in "deciding the issue between Nietzsche and Aristotle"[3] that the future progress of moral philosophy lies.

Many thinkers in the analytic* tradition now take themselves to be philosophical naturalists. This is exemplified by much of the work that has emerged from Cambridge in recent decades, and especially the writings of Edward Craig,* Bernard Williams,* and Huw Price.* But although the movement was partly inspired by Nietzsche, its current practitioners still have much to learn from his approach, particular his realization that this kind of philosophy needs to be supplemented with historical scholarship and more detailed psychological investigation.

Summary

Beyond Good and Evil showcases all of the stylistic features that have made Nietzsche such an influential and admired thinker: it is elegant, entertaining, impassioned, and often humorous. It also contains a clear and concise statement of his central positions on many issues, including morality, epistemology,* psychology, politics, culture, and the arts.

Nietzsche's greatest achievement in *Beyond Good and Evil* is to highlight the deficiencies of our most cherished modern values. He shows that they are the product of outmoded thinking—either religious or metaphysical*—and clears the way for his "philosophers of the future"[4] to legislate new values for humanity to live by. The text also convincingly refutes many influential philosophical achievements, such as Kant's* ethics, Descartes's* epistemology, and Berkeley's* metaphysics. Filled with edifying examples and allusions to classical literature, it rewards almost endless re-reading by both philosophical novices and professional scholars.

Throughout his brief but productive life, Nietzsche strove to be brutally honest and to overcome his own limitations and the assumptions underpinning the society that he was born into. This relentless and uncompromising approach cost him his academic career, and possibly many of his personal relationships as well. However, as this book shows, his determination to be the first philosopher to be "truthful at last" led to the creation of works that were both profound and unsurpassed in their originality. Whether or not a reader ultimately agrees with Nietzsche's conclusions in *Beyond Good and Evil*, they will find engagement with it richly rewarding.

NOTES

1   Friedrich Nietzsche, *Beyond Good and Evil: Prelude to a Philosophy of the Future,* ed. Rolf-Peter Horstmann and Judith Norman, trans. Judith Norman (Cambridge: Cambridge University Press, 2002) introduction, vii.

2   G. E. M. Anscombe, "Modern Moral Philosophy," *Philosophy* 33, no. 124 (1958): 1–19.

3   Alasdair MacIntyre, *After Virtue* (London: Bloomsbury, 2011), 139.

4   Nietzsche, *Beyond Good and Evil,* 39.

GLOSSARY

GLOSSARY OF TERMS

Adaptation: a trait or physical feature that has evolved by means of natural selection.

Ad hominem: a phrase describing arguments against a position that directly attack those who hold a view, rather than anything that is essential to the view itself.

Analytic philosophy: a style of philosophy that has in the last century come to dominate university departments in the English-speaking world. It has its roots in the logical tradition of Gottlob Frege (1848–1925), Bertrand Russell (1872–1970) and G. E. Moore (1873–1958), and emphasizes clarity, literal expression, rigorous rational argument, and the study of language and meaning.

Atheism: the belief that God does not exist.

Categorical Imperative: in Kantian ethics, a universal principle such as "do not lie" which must be obeyed unconditionally by any rational agent.

Cogito ergo sum: literally "I think therefore I am," this proposition has an important role in Descartes's epistemology. Descartes tried to doubt all of his beliefs, but found that it was impossible to doubt this one, because there had to be someone doing the doubting.

Consequentialism: a general term for the family of ethical views such as utilitarianism that regard the moral worth of an action as depending only upon its consequences. It was introduced by Elizabeth Anscombe in 1958.

Continental philosophy: a diverse set of nineteenth- and twentieth-century philosophical traditions united by an interest in the historical and cultural variability of answers to philosophical questions, the limitations of purely scientific modes of inquiry, and the possibility of mobilizing philosophical theory to achieve practical goals.

Darwinism: a world-view centered on the belief that species evolve over time due to the driving force of natural selection.

Deontology: a system of ethics concerned with duty and with absolutely binding principles that must be obeyed regardless of consequences.

Early modern philosophy: a period of philosophy roughly extending across 1500–1800, whose key protagonists include Descartes, Hobbes, Pascal, Leibniz, and Spinoza.

Encyclopédists: a group of Enlightenment thinkers who aimed to collect together all the world's knowledge in a project called the *Encyclopédie*. Its contributors included Diderot, D'Alembert, Voltaire, Rousseau, Montesquieu, and Louise de Jaucourt.

English psychologists: Nietzsche uses this phrase to refer to a group of naturalists including Spencer, Mill, and Rée who sought to reduce human experiences to mechanical phenomena, later making use of the theory of evolution by natural selection supplied by Charles Darwin. "English" denotes a cultural stereotype; the tradition includes thinkers of various nationalities.

Enlightenment: an important historical period in Western civilization that began roughly in the middle of the seventeenth century and continued throughout the eighteenth century. It was characterized by dramatic revolutions in the sciences—culminating in the work of Sir Isaac Newton—and in philosophy, where increasing confidence was placed in the power of reason, experiment, and rational argumentation.

Epistemology: the branch of philosophy dealing with nature of knowledge and the extent of what we know.

Existentialism: a twentieth-century philosophical and literary movement centered on the individual human subject and their experiences and relationship to the world around them. It is most strongly associated with the philosopher Jean-Paul Sartre.

Feminism: an intellectual and political movement that seeks to bring about the end of sexual discrimination, and pursues inquiries into discrimination in relation to issues such as the body, class, employment, reproduction, race, science, human rights, and popular culture.

Foundationalist epistemology: the view that knowledge should be built up from a few sure and certain principles.

Genetic fallacy: the mistaken view that in coming to understand the origins of something we have therefore settled the question of its current value today.

Grand narratives: a term introduced by Jean-François Lyotard in 1984 to denote large-scale theories about the changing understandings of historical and cultural change itself, such as the Enlightenment idea that society progresses over time due to increased scientific knowledge.

Historicism: this is either the view that only history itself can provide us with rational standards for thought, or the epistemological view that our best chance of attaining truth in some particular area of inquiry is by employing historical methods.

Idealism: the metaphysical view that reality is somehow mental in nature and consists of ideas or the activity of the mind.

Jansenism: a seventeenth- and eighteenth-century movement in Catholicism, largely developing in France and Italy, which arose out of the theological problem of reconciling human freedom with the omniscience of a deity.

Judeo-Christian morality: the shared moral inheritance of the Judaic and Christian traditions, as embodied in the Ten Commandments and the teachings of the Old Testament.

Lutheranism: a branch of Christianity that stems from the theological doctrines of Martin Luther (1483–1546), a German monk and Catholic priest.

Marxism: both a methodology for sociological analysis and a theory of historical development. Inspired by the writings of Karl Marx, its traditional emphasis has been on class conflict, the economic determination of behavior, and a systematic and trenchant critique of the capitalist (i.e., profit-oriented) economy.

Medieval philosophy: The period in Western philosophy from the end of the 5th Century to the end of the 15th Century, whose key thinkers include Boethius, Anselm, Abelard, William of Ockham, and perhaps most notably Thomas Aquinas.

Metaphysics: the branch of philosophy dealing with the ultimate nature of being, existence, and reality.

National Socialism (Nazism): a German political movement. Under the leadership of Adolf Hitler, the Nazi party was in power from 1933 until the end of World War II in 1945. The party is widely denounced for its harsh totalitarian methods, and especially for murderous persecution of minorities, particularly the Jews.

Naturalism: an approach to philosophical inquiry that considers only natural, rather than supernatural, explanations of phenomena.

Natural selection: a process by which species change over time due to random variation, inheritance, and selective pressures from the environment.

Parsifal: an opera by Richard Wagner, first produced in 1882, and based on an epic poem by Wolfram von Eschenbach about a religious quest for the Holy Grail.

Perspectivism: the view that the world looks essentially different depending on our character, background experiences, and attitudes, and moreover that there are no reasons to privilege any one of these points of view over another. Particular interpretations of phenomena can thus only come to dominate by force.

Phenomenology: a philosophical approach stemming from the work of Edmund Husserl, which investigates consciousness and lived human experience.

Philology: the branch of knowledge dealing with natural languages and their historical development, especially with reference to classical literature.

Postmodernism: a complex intellectual movement associated with the socially constructed nature of truth and interpretation, the importance of power and its expression in social structures, and skepticism of and attempts to destabilize traditional binary oppositions.

Presbyterianism: a branch of Protestantism stemming from the sixteenth century Swiss Reformation.

Psychoanalysis: both a psychological theory and a therapeutic methodology founded on the idea that unconscious, irrational drives are the true causes of human behavior.

Psychologism: as exemplified by John Locke, this is the view that questions of epistemology are best approached through the study of psychological processes.

Rationalism: the view that reason and not sensory experience is the ultimate foundation for knowledge.

Realpolitik: an approach to politics based on the achievement of concrete objectives, sometimes through questionable means, rather than the intention to act according to abstract ideals.

Romanticism: a Western intellectual movement that began in the late eighteenth century and continued through to the mid-nineteenth century. It influenced contemporary literature, painting, music, architecture, historiography, and philosophy. It is often understood as a reaction to Enlightenment doctrines such as materialism and rationalism, instead emphasizing emotion, creativity, imagination, and individuality as values.

Secularism: the view that religious institutions should not determine the structure or values of society.

Trolley problem: one of a variety of thought experiments in ethics posed by Philippa Foot in 1967. In the simplest case, a choice is given between allowing a runaway train carriage to run over several people trapped on the line, or flipping a switch to transfer it to a siding where it will only run over one trapped person.

Übermensch: the ideal, superior, transcendent future individual that humanity should now aspire to become, as understood by the prophet Zarathustra in Nietzsche's fictional work *Thus Spoke Zarathustra*.

Utilitarianism: an ethical theory that claims that the moral worth of actions should be evaluated solely in terms of how much happiness they lead to. Its founder, Jeremy Bentham, asserted that "it is the greatest happiness of the greatest number that is the measure of right and wrong."

Virtue ethics: an approach to moral philosophy stemming from the work of Aristotle, whose moral philosophy focuses on the good life for human beings and the development of the virtues (such as courage, honesty and temperance) as a means to this end.

PEOPLE MENTIONED IN THE TEXT

Theodor Adorno (1903–69) was a German philosopher, known for his writings on sociology, psychology, and musical theory.

Aristotle (384–322 B.C.E.) was an Ancient Greek philosopher. He wrote treatises on a vast range of subjects in both the arts and sciences, and pioneered the systematic study of biology and formal logic. His philosophy and cosmology dominated the intellectual landscape of the West for many centuries in the Middle Ages. In terms of influence, only Plato rivals him.

Peter Abelard (1079–1142) was a French theologian, philosopher and poet, best known for his use of dialect and his attempts to solve the problem of universals.

Elizabeth (G. E. M.) Anscombe (1919–2001) was a British philosopher. She was the executor of the philosopher Ludwig Wittgenstein's literary estate, and best remembered for her influential 1958 article "Modern Moral Philosophy" and her 1957 work *Intention*.

Saint Anselm of Canterbury (1033–1109) was an Italian theologian and philosopher. Best known as the father of Scholasticism and for his "ontological argument" for the existence of God, he exerted a strong influence over medieval philosophy.

Saint Thomas Aquinas (1225–74) was an Italian Dominican theologian and philosopher. He attempted to synthesize Christianity with the works of Aristotle and is considered by many to be the greatest medieval philosopher.

Ludwig van Beethoven (1770–1827) was a celebrated German composer and pianist. He wrote many of his most admired works whilst suffering from a loss of hearing which would become complete by the last decade of his life.

George Berkeley (1685–1753) was an Irish philosopher, scientist, and Anglican bishop. He is best known for his idealism and empiricism, and his work on vision.

Jeremy Bentham (1748–1832) was a British philosopher and social reformer. He is chiefly known for being an early proponent of utilitarianism, the view that morality always requires the pursuit of the "greatest happiness of the greatest number."

Otto von Bismarck (1815–98) was prime minister of Prussia and the first chancellor of the German Empire. After establishing the empire in 1871, his pragmatic foreign policies enabled him to keep the peace in Europe for two decades, though he was criticized for his authoritarian domestic reforms.

Georg Brandes (1842–1927) was an influential Danish critic and scholar. He was amongst the first to lecture on Nietzsche's work.

Maudemarie Clarke is an American philosopher. She specializes in nineteenth-century philosophy and is mainly known for her work on Nietzsche.

Edward Craig (b. 1942) is a retired Cambridge philosopher and cricketer. He is the editor of the 10-volume *Routledge Encyclopedia of Philosophy*.

Charles Darwin (1809–82) was an English naturalist. He is most famous for being the first to articulate scientifically the proposition that all life is descended from a single source in a process that is driven by the mechanisms of natural selection. His work influenced virtually all aspects of the biological sciences.

Democritus (circa 460–circa 370 B.C.E.) was an Ancient Greek philosopher. He was known for his doctrine of atomism, wherein he tried to account for the natural world as made up of indivisible atoms, and for his emphasizing the value of cheerfulness.

René Descartes (1596–1650) was a French mathematician, scientist, and philosopher. Known as the father of modern philosophy, amongst his many achievements was to lay the foundations of analytic geometry, to make advances in epistemology with his method of radical doubt, to inspire generations of dualist theorists in the philosophy of mind, and to help lay the theoretical foundations for modern science.

Gilles Deleuze (1925–95) was an influential French philosopher. He attempted to develop a new metaphysical system that could accommodate the complexities of contemporary mathematics and science.

Denis Diderot (1713–84) was a philosopher of the French Enlightenment. He is best known for being the chief editor of the *Encyclopédie*, an attempt to systematically set out all of the world's scientific knowledge, and his many plays, poems, and novels, such as *Rameau's Nephew*.

Ralph Waldo Emerson (1803–82) was an American essayist and poet. He was a leading proponent of New England Transcendentalism, an idealist philosophical movement based on belief in the innate goodness of man and the primacy of intuition over rational methods.

Philippa Foot (1920–2010) was a British philosopher. She was a noted proponent of virtue ethics, a tradition stemming from Aristotle.

Elizabeth Förster-Nietzsche (1846–1935) was Nietzsche's sister. For many years she was the sole executor of his literary estate.

Michel Foucault (1926–84) was a French philosopher and social theorist. Heavily influenced by Nietzsche, he wrote extensively about power and its expression by social institutions throughout history. He also wrote histories of madness, sexuality, and punishment.

William K. Frankena (1908–94) was an American moral philosopher who worked in the analytic tradition; his main research interest was ethics.

Gottlob Frege (1848–1925) was a German mathematician and philosopher. Though mainly working on the foundations of mathematics, his writings on language later became hugely influential and he is now regarded as one of the founders of analytic philosophy.

Sigmund Freud (1856–1939) was an influential Austrian psychologist and medical doctor. He is best known as the founder of psychoanalysis, a school with both theoretical and therapeutic doctrines that stressed the importance of unconscious, irrational drives and the experiences of childhood.

Johann Wolfgang von Goethe (1749–1832) was an influential German writer and statesman. He is best known for his tragic play *Faust*.

Martin Heidegger (1889–1976) was an important German philosopher. He is associated with the phenomenological and existentialist traditions, and best known for his masterpiece *Being and Time*.

Heinrich Heine (1797–1856) was a German author and poet. His literary reputation was established by *The Book of Songs* in 1827.

Heraclitus (circa 540–circa 480 B.C.E.) was a Greek philosopher. He argued that fire was the most fundamental material principle of the universe, and was known for emphasizing that reality is always in a state of flux.

David Hume (1711–76) was an influential Scottish philosopher. He is known for his skeptical attitude towards received beliefs in philosophy and religion, his development of empiricism, and his attempts to ground metaphysical principles in human nature and habit rather than rational argumentation.

Christopher Janaway is professor of philosophy at the University of Southampton. He has published work on Schopenhauer and Nietzsche.

James Joyce (1882–1941) was an Irish writer and perhaps the most acclaimed novelist of the twentieth century. He is best known for his stream-of-consciousness prose style and his long works, such as *Ulysses* and *Finnegan's Wake*.

Immanuel Kant (1724–1804) was a German Enlightenment philosopher. A towering figure in modern philosophy, he contributed to a wide range of areas including ethics, epistemology, metaphysics, and aesthetics, and sought to synthesize the rationalist and empiricist traditions of the early modern period.

Walter Kaufmann (1921–80) was a German-American philosopher, translator and noted Nietzsche scholar. He provided many of the first translations of Nietzsche's key works, and was instrumental in the increasing interest in his writings from the mid-twentieth century onwards.

Søren Kierkegaard (1813–55) was a Danish philosopher, theologian, and social critic. A founder of existentialism, he was interested in concrete human experiences and attempted to rejuvenate the Christian faith.

Friedrich Albert Lange (1828–75) was a German philosopher. He was instrumental in the development of neo-Kantianism and German social democratic thought.

Brian Leiter (b. 1963) is an American philosopher and legal scholar. He is primarily known for his work on Nietzsche and his legal philosophy.

Alasdair MacIntyre (b. 1929) is an influential Scottish philosopher. He is primarily known for his historical approach to moral philosophy, his Aristotelian and Thomistic commitments, and his trenchant critiques of liberal values.

Karl Marx (1818–83) was a highly influential economist and social theorist. Marxist theory is derived from his works, notably *Capital* (1867–94) and *The Communist Manifesto* (1848).

John Stuart Mill (1806–73) was an English philosopher and important liberal thinker. He is best known for his development of utilitarianism, but he also made contributions to the philosophy of science and served as a member of parliament.

Wolfgang Amadeus Mozart (1756–91) was an Austrian composer. His work spanned a variety of classical genres and he is widely regarded as one of the greatest composers in the history of Western music.

Plato (circa 429–347 B.C.E.) was an ancient Greek philosopher and perhaps the most influential philosopher who ever lived. He was famous for writing in dialogues, and for discussing the doctrine of the forms. His works largely center on conversations with a character called Socrates, based on the historical philosopher who was his teacher.

Huw Price (b. 1953) is an Australian philosopher based at Trinity College, Cambridge. He is known for his work on time, and his naturalist and pragmatist approaches in the philosophy of language.

Paul Rée (1849–1901) was a philosopher and contemporary of Nietzsche. The two had previously been friends, though Nietzsche felt Rée had betrayed him over the affections of Lou Andreas-Salomé.

Erwin Rohde (1845–98) was a German classical scholar. His work *Psyche* made a substantial contribution to knowledge of Greek ideas and rituals concerning the soul.

Friedrich Wilhelm Ritschl (1806–76) was a German classical scholar. He is most notable for his work on the Roman playwright Plautus.

François De La Rochefoucauld (1613–80) was a classical French author, nobleman, and political activist. He is primarily known for his *Maxims*, short aphorisms containing a witty or polemical observation concerning some social or philosophical topic.

Bertrand Russell (1872–1970) was a British mathematician, social critic, and philosopher. He produced influential work in mathematical logic and was one of the founders of the analytical school of philosophy.

Jean-Paul Sartre (1905–80) was a well-known French philosopher, writer, and public intellectual. In philosophy, he is best known as the founder of the existentialist movement.

Arthur Schopenhauer (1788–1860) was a German philosopher, best known for his 1818 book *The World as Will and Representation*. Generally regarded as a pessimistic nihilist, he advocated the use of culture and the arts as an escape from the suffering inherent in human existence.

George Bernard Shaw (1856–1950) was an Irish dramatist and literary critic. In 1925 he won the Nobel Prize for Literature.

Peter Sloterdijk (b. 1947) is a German philosopher, cultural critic, and television presenter. His magnum opus *Spheres* is a three-volume work about the spaces in which human beings attempt to live.

Adam Smith (1723–90) was a philosopher and economist of the Scottish Enlightenment. He is primarily known for his 1776 work *An Inquiry into the Nature and Causes of the Wealth of Nations*, the first systematic treatise on political economy.

Socrates (circa 470–399 B.C.E.) was an ancient Greek philosopher. Though he left no written works, and is now known only through the works of Plato, Xenophon, and Aristophanes, his influence was so strong that he is widely regarded as the founder of Western philosophy. He was executed by the state of Athens for impiety and corrupting the youth.

Herbert Spencer (1820–1903) was an English philosopher. He was an important exponent of evolutionary theory and utilitarian ideas.

Baruch Spinoza (1632–77) was a Dutch Jewish philosopher. He was one of the foremost exponents of rationalism and a central figure in the Enlightenment philosophical movement.

Stendhal (1783–1842) was the pen name of French author Marie-Henri Beyle. He is chiefly known for his works *The Red and the Black* (1830) and *The Charterhouse of Parma* (1839).

Voltaire (1694–1778) was the pen name of François-Marie d'Arouet, a French writer, activist, and Enlightenment philosopher. He was known for emphasizing the power of reason and empirical science, and the value of free speech.

Richard Wagner (1813–83) was a German composer, director, and conductor, best known for his operas, such as *Tristan and Isolde, The Ring of the Nibelung*, and *Parsifal*.

Joseph Viktor Widmann (1842–1911) was a Swiss writer and critic, and editor of the Swiss daily newspaper *Der Bund* from 1880 to 1910.

Ulrich von Wilamowitz-Möllendorff (1848–1931) was a German classical philologist. Primarily known as an authority on Ancient Greek literature, he was the dominant classical scholar of his era.

Bernard Williams (1929–2003) was a leading twentieth-century moral philosopher. He opposed the reduction of ethics to abstract systems of rules, and contributed to debates about moral psychology and personal identity.

WORKS CITED

WORKS CITED

Acampora, Christa Davis, and Keith Ansell Pearson. *Nietzsche's Beyond Good and Evil*. London: Continuum, 2011.

Anscombe, G. E. M. "Modern Moral Philosophy." *Philosophy* 33, no. 124 (1958): 1–19.

Brobjer, Thomas H. *Nietzsche's Philosophical Context*. Chicago: University of Illinois Press, 2008.

Copleston, Frederick. *A History of Philosophy*, Volume 7: *18th and 19th Century German Philosophy*. London: Bloomsbury, 2013.

Deleuze, Gilles. *Nietzsche and Philosophy*. Translated by Hugh Tomlinson. London: Athlone, 1983.

Descartes, René. *Meditations on First Philosophy*. Translated and edited by John Cottingham. Cambridge: Cambridge University Press, 1996.

Diamond, Jared. *The World Until Yesterday: What Can We Learn From Traditional Societies?* New York: Penguin, 2012.

Foot, Philippa. "Nietzsche's Immoralism." In *Nietzsche, Genealogy, Morality*, edited by Richard Schacht. Berkeley: University of California Press, 1994.

Foucault, Michel. "Truth, Power, Self: An Interview with Michel Foucault." In *Technologies of the Self,* edited by Luther H. Martin, Huck Gutman and Patrick Hutton. London: Tavistock, 1988.

Frankena, William K. "Review: MacIntyre and Modern Morality." *Ethics* 93, no. 3 (1983): 579–87.

Frege, Gottlob. *The Foundations of Arithmetic.* Translated by J. L. Austin. Oxford: Basil Blackwell, 1980.

Gillespie, Michael Allen and Keegan F. Callanan. "On the Genealogy of Morals.*"* In *A Companion to Friedrich Nietzsche*, edited by Paul Bishop. New York: Camden House, 2012.

Janaway, Christopher. *Beyond Selflessness: Reading Nietzsche's Genealogy.* Oxford: Oxford University Press, 2007.

Jones, Ernest. *The Life and Work of Sigmund Freud*. Vol. II. New York: Basic Books, 1953.

Kant, Immanuel. *Practical Philosophy*. Translated by Mary Gregor. Cambridge: Cambridge University Press, 1996.

Kaufmann, Walter. *Nietzsche: Philosopher, Psychologist, Antichrist*. New Jersey: Princeton University Press, 1974.

Lange, Friedrich Albert. *The History of Materialism and Criticism of Its Present Importance*. Translated by Ernest Chester Thomas. Charleston: Nabu Press, 2011.

MacIntyre, Alasdair. *After Virtue*. London: Bloomsbury, 2011.

Mill, John Stuart. *Utilitarianism*. Cambridge: Cambridge University Press, 2014.

Nietzsche, Friedrich. *The Anti-Christ, Ecce Homo, Twilight of the Idols*. Translated by Judith Norman. Cambridge: Cambridge University Press, 2005.

Beyond Good and Evil. Edited by Rolf-Peter Horstmann and Judith Norman. Translated by Judith Norman. Cambridge: Cambridge University Press, 2002.

The Birth of Tragedy. Edited by Raymond Geuss and Ronald Speirs. Translated by Ronald Speirs. Cambridge: Cambridge University Press, 1999.

Daybreak. Edited by Maudemarie Clark and Brian Leiter. Translated by R. J. Hollingdale. Cambridge: Cambridge University Press, 1997.

The Gay Science. Edited by Bernard Williams. Translated by Josefine Nauckhoff. Cambridge: Cambridge University Press, 2001.

Human, All Too Human. Translated by R. J. Hollingdale. Cambridge: Cambridge University Press, 1996.

On the Genealogy of Morality. Translated by Maudemarie Clark and Alan Swensen. Indianapolis: Hackett, 1998.

Untimely Meditations. Edited by Daniel Breazeale. Translated by R. J. Hollingdale. Cambridge: Cambridge University Press, 1997.

Prange, Martine. "Beyond Good and Evil". In *A Companion to Friedrich Nietzsche*, edited by Paul Bishop. New York: Camden House, 2012.

Rée, Paul. *Basic Writings*. Edited and translated by Robin Small. Urbana: University of Illinois Press, 2003.

Russell, Bertrand. *History of Western Philosophy*. New York: Routledge, 1996.

Safranski, Rüdiger. *Nietzsche: A Philosophical Biography*. Translated by Shelley Frisch. London: Granta Books, 2002.

Sloterdijk, Peter. *Critique of Cynical Reason*. Translated by Michael Eldred. Minnesota: University of Minnesota Press, 1988.

Valente, Joseph. "Beyond Truth and Freedom: The New Faith of Joyce and Nietzsche." *James Joyce Quarterly* 25, no. 1 (1987): 87–103.

Widmann, Joseph Viktor. "Nietzsche's Dangerous Book." *New Nietzsche Studies* 4 (2000): 195–200.

Williams, Bernard. *Truth and Truthfulness.* Princeton: Princeton University Press, 2002.

Ethics and the Limits of Philosophy. Abingdon: Routledge, 2011.

THE MACAT LIBRARY
BY DISCIPLINE

The Macat Library By Discipline

AFRICANA STUDIES

Chinua Achebe's *An Image of Africa: Racism in Conrad's Heart of Darkness*
W. E. B. Du Bois's *The Souls of Black Folk*
Zora Neale Huston's *Characteristics of Negro Expression*
Martin Luther King Jr's *Why We Can't Wait*
Toni Morrison's *Playing in the Dark: Whiteness in the American Literary Imagination*

ANTHROPOLOGY

Arjun Appadurai's *Modernity at Large: Cultural Dimensions of Globalisation*
Philippe Ariès's *Centuries of Childhood*
Franz Boas's *Race, Language and Culture*
Kim Chan & Renée Mauborgne's *Blue Ocean Strategy*
Jared Diamond's *Guns, Germs & Steel: the Fate of Human Societies*
Jared Diamond's *Collapse: How Societies Choose to Fail or Survive*
E. E. Evans-Pritchard's *Witchcraft, Oracles and Magic Among the Azande*
James Ferguson's *The Anti-Politics Machine*
Clifford Geertz's *The Interpretation of Cultures*
David Graeber's *Debt: the First 5000 Years*
Karen Ho's *Liquidated: An Ethnography of Wall Street*
Geert Hofstede's *Culture's Consequences: Comparing Values, Behaviors, Institutes and Organizations across Nations*
Claude Lévi-Strauss's *Structural Anthropology*
Jay Macleod's *Ain't No Makin' It: Aspirations and Attainment in a Low-Income Neighborhood*
Saba Mahmood's *The Politics of Piety: The Islamic Revival and the Feminist Subjec*t
Marcel Mauss's *The Gift*

BUSINESS

Jean Lave & Etienne Wenger's *Situated Learning*
Theodore Levitt's *Marketing Myopia*
Burton G. Malkiel's *A Random Walk Down Wall Street*
Douglas McGregor's *The Human Side of Enterprise*
Michael Porter's *Competitive Strategy: Creating and Sustaining Superior Performance*
John Kotter's *Leading Change*
C. K. Prahalad & Gary Hamel's *The Core Competence of the Corporation*

CRIMINOLOGY

Michelle Alexander's *The New Jim Crow: Mass Incarceration in the Age of Colorblindness*
Michael R. Gottfredson & Travis Hirschi's *A General Theory of Crime*
Richard Herrnstein & Charles A. Murray's *The Bell Curve: Intelligence and Class Structure in American Life*
Elizabeth Loftus's *Eyewitness Testimony*
Jay Macleod's *Ain't No Makin' It: Aspirations and Attainment in a Low-Income Neighborhood*
Philip Zimbardo's *The Lucifer Effect*

ECONOMICS

Janet Abu-Lughod's *Before European Hegemony*
Ha-Joon Chang's *Kicking Away the Ladder*
David Brion Davis's *The Problem of Slavery in the Age of Revolution*
Milton Friedman's *The Role of Monetary Policy*
Milton Friedman's *Capitalism and Freedom*
David Graeber's *Debt: the First 5000 Years*
Friedrich Hayek's *The Road to Serfdom*
Karen Ho's *Liquidated: An Ethnography of Wall Street*

John Maynard Keynes's *The General Theory of Employment, Interest and Money*
Charles P. Kindleberger's *Manias, Panics and Crashes*
Robert Lucas's *Why Doesn't Capital Flow from Rich to Poor Countries?*
Burton G. Malkiel's *A Random Walk Down Wall Street*
Thomas Robert Malthus's *An Essay on the Principle of Population*
Karl Marx's *Capital*
Thomas Piketty's *Capital in the Twenty-First Century*
Amartya Sen's *Development as Freedom*
Adam Smith's *The Wealth of Nations*
Nassim Nicholas Taleb's *The Black Swan: The Impact of the Highly Improbable*
Amos Tversky's & Daniel Kahneman's *Judgment under Uncertainty: Heuristics and Biases*
Mahbub Ul Haq's *Reflections on Human Development*
Max Weber's *The Protestant Ethic and the Spirit of Capitalism*

FEMINISM AND GENDER STUDIES

Judith Butler's *Gender Trouble*
Simone De Beauvoir's *The Second Sex*
Michel Foucault's *History of Sexuality*
Betty Friedan's *The Feminine Mystique*
Saba Mahmood's *The Politics of Piety: The Islamic Revival and the Feminist Subject*
Joan Wallach Scott's *Gender and the Politics of History*
Mary Wollstonecraft's *A Vindication of the Rights of Woman*
Virginia Woolf's *A Room of One's Own*

GEOGRAPHY

The Brundtland Report's *Our Common Future*
Rachel Carson's *Silent Spring*
Charles Darwin's *On the Origin of Species*
James Ferguson's *The Anti-Politics Machine*
Jane Jacobs's *The Death and Life of Great American Cities*
James Lovelock's *Gaia: A New Look at Life on Earth*
Amartya Sen's *Development as Freedom*
Mathis Wackernagel & William Rees's *Our Ecological Footprint*

HISTORY

Janet Abu-Lughod's *Before European Hegemony*
Benedict Anderson's *Imagined Communities*
Bernard Bailyn's *The Ideological Origins of the American Revolution*
Hanna Batatu's *The Old Social Classes And The Revolutionary Movements Of Iraq*
Christopher Browning's *Ordinary Men: Reserve Police Batallion 101 and the Final Solution in Poland*
Edmund Burke's *Reflections on the Revolution in France*
William Cronon's *Nature's Metropolis: Chicago And The Great West*
Alfred W. Crosby's *The Columbian Exchange*
Hamid Dabashi's *Iran: A People Interrupted*
David Brion Davis's *The Problem of Slavery in the Age of Revolution*
Nathalie Zemon Davis's *The Return of Martin Guerre*
Jared Diamond's *Guns, Germs & Steel: the Fate of Human Societies*
Frank Dikotter's *Mao's Great Famine*
John W Dower's *War Without Mercy: Race And Power In The Pacific War*
W. E. B. Du Bois's *The Souls of Black Folk*
Richard J. Evans's *In Defence of History*
Lucien Febvre's *The Problem of Unbelief in the 16th Century*
Sheila Fitzpatrick's *Everyday Stalinism*

The Macat Library By Discipline

Eric Foner's *Reconstruction: America's Unfinished Revolution, 1863-1877*
Michel Foucault's *Discipline and Punish*
Michel Foucault's *History of Sexuality*
Francis Fukuyama's *The End of History and the Last Man*
John Lewis Gaddis's *We Now Know: Rethinking Cold War History*
Ernest Gellner's *Nations and Nationalism*
Eugene Genovese's *Roll, Jordan, Roll: The World the Slaves Made*
Carlo Ginzburg's *The Night Battles*
Daniel Goldhagen's *Hitler's Willing Executioners*
Jack Goldstone's *Revolution and Rebellion in the Early Modern World*
Antonio Gramsci's *The Prison Notebooks*
Alexander Hamilton, John Jay & James Madison's *The Federalist Papers*
Christopher Hill's *The World Turned Upside Down*
Carole Hillenbrand's *The Crusades: Islamic Perspectives*
Thomas Hobbes's *Leviathan*
Eric Hobsbawm's *The Age Of Revolution*
John A. Hobson's *Imperialism: A Study*
Albert Hourani's *History of the Arab Peoples*
Samuel P. Huntington's *The Clash of Civilizations and the Remaking of World Order*
C. L. R. James's *The Black Jacobins*
Tony Judt's *Postwar: A History of Europe Since 1945*
Ernst Kantorowicz's *The King's Two Bodies: A Study in Medieval Political Theology*
Paul Kennedy's *The Rise and Fall of the Great Powers*
Ian Kershaw's *The "Hitler Myth": Image and Reality in the Third Reich*
John Maynard Keynes's *The General Theory of Employment, Interest and Money*
Charles P. Kindleberger's *Manias, Panics and Crashes*
Martin Luther King Jr's *Why We Can't Wait*
Henry Kissinger's *World Order: Reflections on the Character of Nations and the Course of History*
Thomas Kuhn's *The Structure of Scientific Revolutions*
Georges Lefebvre's *The Coming of the French Revolution*
John Locke's *Two Treatises of Government*
Niccolò Machiavelli's *The Prince*
Thomas Robert Malthus's *An Essay on the Principle of Population*
Mahmood Mamdani's *Citizen and Subject: Contemporary Africa And The Legacy Of Late Colonialism*
Karl Marx's *Capital*
Stanley Milgram's *Obedience to Authority*
John Stuart Mill's *On Liberty*
Thomas Paine's *Common Sense*
Thomas Paine's *Rights of Man*
Geoffrey Parker's *Global Crisis: War, Climate Change and Catastrophe in the Seventeenth Century*
Jonathan Riley-Smith's *The First Crusade and the Idea of Crusading*
Jean-Jacques Rousseau's *The Social Contract*
Joan Wallach Scott's *Gender and the Politics of History*
Theda Skocpol's *States and Social Revolutions*
Adam Smith's *The Wealth of Nations*
Timothy Snyder's *Bloodlands: Europe Between Hitler and Stalin*
Sun Tzu's *The Art of War*
Keith Thomas's *Religion and the Decline of Magic*
Thucydides's *The History of the Peloponnesian War*
Frederick Jackson Turner's *The Significance of the Frontier in American History*
Odd Arne Westad's *The Global Cold War: Third World Interventions And The Making Of Our Times*

LITERATURE

Chinua Achebe's *An Image of Africa: Racism in Conrad's Heart of Darkness*
Roland Barthes's *Mythologies*
Homi K. Bhabha's *The Location of Culture*
Judith Butler's *Gender Trouble*
Simone De Beauvoir's *The Second Sex*
Ferdinand De Saussure's *Course In General Linguistics*
T. S. Eliot's *The Sacred Wood: Essays on Poetry and Criticism*
Zora Neale Huston's *Characteristics of Negro Expression*
Toni Morrison's *Playing in the Dark: Whiteness in the American Literary Imagination*
Edward Said's *Orientalism*
Gayatri Chakravorty Spivak's *Can the Subaltern Speak?*
Mary Wollstonecraft's *A Vindication of the Rights of Woman*
Virginia Woolf's *A Room of One's Own*

PHILOSOPHY

Elizabeth Anscombe's *Modern Moral Philosophy*
Hannah Arendt's *The Human Condition*
Aristotle's *Metaphysics*
Aristotle's *Nicomachean Ethics*
Edmund Gettier's *Is Justified True Belief Knowledge?*
Georg Wilhelm Friedrich Hegel's *Phenomenology of Spirit*
David Hume's *Dialogues Concerning Natural Religion*
David Hume's *The Enquiry for Human Understanding*
Immanuel Kant's *Religion within the Boundaries of Mere Reason*
Immanuel Kant's *Critique of Pure Reason*
Søren Kierkegaard's *The Sickness Unto Death*
Søren Kierkegaard's *Fear and Trembling*
C. S. Lewis's *The Abolition of Man*
Alasdair MacIntyre's *After Virtue*
Marcus Aurelius's *Meditations*
Friedrich Nietzsche's *On the Genealogy of Morality*
Friedrich Nietzsche's *Beyond Good and Evil*
Plato's *Republic*
Plato's *Symposium*
Jean-Jacques Rousseau's *The Social Contract*
Gilbert Ryle's *The Concept of Mind*
Baruch Spinoza's *Ethics*
Sun Tzu's *The Art of War*
Ludwig Wittgenstein's *Philosophical Investigations*

POLITICS

Benedict Anderson's *Imagined Communities*
Aristotle's *Politics*
Bernard Bailyn's *The Ideological Origins of the American Revolution*
Edmund Burke's *Reflections on the Revolution in France*
John C. Calhoun's *A Disquisition on Government*
Ha-Joon Chang's *Kicking Away the Ladder*
Hamid Dabashi's *Iran: A People Interrupted*
Hamid Dabashi's *Theology of Discontent: The Ideological Foundation of the Islamic Revolution in Iran*
Robert Dahl's *Democracy and its Critics*
Robert Dahl's *Who Governs?*
David Brion Davis's *The Problem of Slavery in the Age of Revolution*

The Macat Library By Discipline

Alexis De Tocqueville's *Democracy in America*
James Ferguson's *The Anti-Politics Machine*
Frank Dikotter's *Mao's Great Famine*
Sheila Fitzpatrick's *Everyday Stalinism*
Eric Foner's *Reconstruction: America's Unfinished Revolution, 1863-1877*
Milton Friedman's *Capitalism and Freedom*
Francis Fukuyama's *The End of History and the Last Man*
John Lewis Gaddis's *We Now Know: Rethinking Cold War History*
Ernest Gellner's *Nations and Nationalism*
David Graeber's *Debt: the First 5000 Years*
Antonio Gramsci's *The Prison Notebooks*
Alexander Hamilton, John Jay & James Madison's *The Federalist Papers*
Friedrich Hayek's *The Road to Serfdom*
Christopher Hill's *The World Turned Upside Down*
Thomas Hobbes's *Leviathan*
John A. Hobson's *Imperialism: A Study*
Samuel P. Huntington's *The Clash of Civilizations and the Remaking of World Order*
Tony Judt's *Postwar: A History of Europe Since 1945*
David C. Kang's *China Rising: Peace, Power and Order in East Asia*
Paul Kennedy's *The Rise and Fall of Great Powers*
Robert Keohane's *After Hegemony*
Martin Luther King Jr.'s *Why We Can't Wait*
Henry Kissinger's *World Order: Reflections on the Character of Nations and the Course of History*
John Locke's *Two Treatises of Government*
Niccolò Machiavelli's *The Prince*
Thomas Robert Malthus's *An Essay on the Principle of Population*
Mahmood Mamdani's *Citizen and Subject: Contemporary Africa And The Legacy Of Late Colonialism*
Karl Marx's *Capital*
John Stuart Mill's *On Liberty*
John Stuart Mill's *Utilitarianism*
Hans Morgenthau's *Politics Among Nations*
Thomas Paine's *Common Sense*
Thomas Paine's *Rights of Man*
Thomas Piketty's *Capital in the Twenty-First Century*
Robert D. Putman's *Bowling Alone*
John Rawls's *Theory of Justice*
Jean-Jacques Rousseau's *The Social Contract*
Theda Skocpol's *States and Social Revolutions*
Adam Smith's *The Wealth of Nations*
Sun Tzu's *The Art of War*
Henry David Thoreau's *Civil Disobedience*
Thucydides's *The History of the Peloponnesian War*
Kenneth Waltz's *Theory of International Politics*
Max Weber's *Politics as a Vocation*
Odd Arne Westad's *The Global Cold War: Third World Interventions And The Making Of Our Times*

POSTCOLONIAL STUDIES

Roland Barthes's *Mythologies*
Frantz Fanon's *Black Skin, White Masks*
Homi K. Bhabha's *The Location of Culture*
Gustavo Gutiérrez's *A Theology of Liberation*
Edward Said's *Orientalism*
Gayatri Chakravorty Spivak's *Can the Subaltern Speak?*

PSYCHOLOGY

Gordon Allport's *The Nature of Prejudice*
Alan Baddeley & Graham Hitch's *Aggression: A Social Learning Analysis*
Albert Bandura's *Aggression: A Social Learning Analysis*
Leon Festinger's *A Theory of Cognitive Dissonance*
Sigmund Freud's *The Interpretation of Dreams*
Betty Friedan's *The Feminine Mystique*
Michael R. Gottfredson & Travis Hirschi's *A General Theory of Crime*
Eric Hoffer's *The True Believer: Thoughts on the Nature of Mass Movements*
William James's *Principles of Psychology*
Elizabeth Loftus's *Eyewitness Testimony*
A. H. Maslow's *A Theory of Human Motivation*
Stanley Milgram's *Obedience to Authority*
Steven Pinker's *The Better Angels of Our Nature*
Oliver Sacks's *The Man Who Mistook His Wife For a Hat*
Richard Thaler & Cass Sunstein's *Nudge: Improving Decisions About Health, Wealth and Happiness*
Amos Tversky's *Judgment under Uncertainty: Heuristics and Biases*
Philip Zimbardo's *The Lucifer Effect*

SCIENCE

Rachel Carson's *Silent Spring*
William Cronon's *Nature's Metropolis: Chicago And The Great West*
Alfred W. Crosby's *The Columbian Exchange*
Charles Darwin's *On the Origin of Species*
Richard Dawkin's *The Selfish Gene*
Thomas Kuhn's *The Structure of Scientific Revolutions*
Geoffrey Parker's *Global Crisis: War, Climate Change and Catastrophe in the Seventeenth Century*
Mathis Wackernagel & William Rees's *Our Ecological Footprint*

SOCIOLOGY

Michelle Alexander's *The New Jim Crow: Mass Incarceration in the Age of Colorblindness*
Gordon Allport's *The Nature of Prejudice*
Albert Bandura's *Aggression: A Social Learning Analysis*
Hanna Batatu's *The Old Social Classes And The Revolutionary Movements Of Iraq*
Ha-Joon Chang's *Kicking Away the Ladder*
W. E. B. Du Bois's *The Souls of Black Folk*
Émile Durkheim's *On Suicide*
Frantz Fanon's *Black Skin, White Masks*
Frantz Fanon's *The Wretched of the Earth*
Eric Foner's *Reconstruction: America's Unfinished Revolution, 1863-1877*
Eugene Genovese's *Roll, Jordan, Roll: The World the Slaves Made*
Jack Goldstone's *Revolution and Rebellion in the Early Modern World*
Antonio Gramsci's *The Prison Notebooks*
Richard Herrnstein & Charles A Murray's *The Bell Curve: Intelligence and Class Structure in American Life*
Eric Hoffer's *The True Believer: Thoughts on the Nature of Mass Movements*
Jane Jacobs's *The Death and Life of Great American Cities*
Robert Lucas's *Why Doesn't Capital Flow from Rich to Poor Countries?*
Jay Macleod's *Ain't No Makin' It: Aspirations and Attainment in a Low Income Neighborhood*
Elaine May's *Homeward Bound: American Families in the Cold War Era*
Douglas McGregor's *The Human Side of Enterprise*
C. Wright Mills's *The Sociological Imagination*

The Macat Library By Discipline

Thomas Piketty's *Capital in the Twenty-First Century*
Robert D. Putman's *Bowling Alone*
David Riesman's *The Lonely Crowd: A Study of the Changing American Character*
Edward Said's *Orientalism*
Joan Wallach Scott's *Gender and the Politics of History*
Theda Skocpol's *States and Social Revolutions*
Max Weber's *The Protestant Ethic and the Spirit of Capitalism*

THEOLOGY

Augustine's *Confessions*
Benedict's *Rule of St Benedict*
Gustavo Gutiérrez's *A Theology of Liberation*
Carole Hillenbrand's *The Crusades: Islamic Perspectives*
David Hume's *Dialogues Concerning Natural Religion*
Immanuel Kant's *Religion within the Boundaries of Mere Reason*
Ernst Kantorowicz's *The King's Two Bodies: A Study in Medieval Political Theology*
Søren Kierkegaard's *The Sickness Unto Death*
C. S. Lewis's *The Abolition of Man*
Saba Mahmood's *The Politics of Piety: The Islamic Revival and the Feminist Subject*
Baruch Spinoza's *Ethics*
Keith Thomas's *Religion and the Decline of Magic*

COMING SOON

Chris Argyris's *The Individual and the Organisation*
Seyla Benhabib's *The Rights of Others*
Walter Benjamin's *The Work Of Art in the Age of Mechanical Reproduction*
John Berger's *Ways of Seeing*
Pierre Bourdieu's *Outline of a Theory of Practice*
Mary Douglas's *Purity and Danger*
Roland Dworkin's *Taking Rights Seriously*
James G. March's *Exploration and Exploitation in Organisational Learning*
Ikujiro Nonaka's *A Dynamic Theory of Organizational Knowledge Creation*
Griselda Pollock's *Vision and Difference*
Amartya Sen's *Inequality Re-Examined*
Susan Sontag's *On Photography*
Yasser Tabbaa's *The Transformation of Islamic Art*
Ludwig von Mises's *Theory of Money and Credit*

Macat Disciplines

Access the greatest ideas and thinkers across entire disciplines, including

FEMINISM, GENDER AND QUEER STUDIES

Simone De Beauvoir's
The Second Sex

Michel Foucault's
History of Sexuality

Betty Friedan's
The Feminine Mystique

Saba Mahmood's
*The Politics of Piety:
The Islamic Revival and
the Feminist Subject*

Joan Wallach Scott's
*Gender and the
Politics of History*

Mary Wollstonecraft's
*A Vindication of the
Rights of Woman*

Virginia Woolf's
A Room of One's Own

Judith Butler's
Gender Trouble

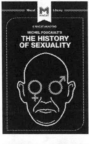

Macat analyses are available from all good bookshops and libraries.

Access hundreds of analyses through one, multimedia tool.

Join free for one month **library.macat.com**

Macat Disciplines

Access the greatest ideas and thinkers across entire disciplines, including

CRIMINOLOGY

Michelle Alexander's
*The New Jim Crow:
Mass Incarceration in the
Age of Colorblindness*

**Michael R. Gottfredson
& Travis Hirschi's**
A General Theory of Crime

Elizabeth Loftus's
Eyewitness Testimony

**Richard Herrnstein
& Charles A. Murray's**
*The Bell Curve: Intelligence and
Class Structure in American Life*

Jay Macleod's
*Ain't No Makin' It:
Aspirations and Attainment in a
Low-Income Neighborhood*

Philip Zimbardo's
The Lucifer Effect

Macat analyses are available from all good bookshops and libraries.

Access hundreds of analyses through one, multimedia tool.
Join free for one month **library.macat.com**

Macat Disciplines

Access the greatest ideas and thinkers across entire disciplines, including

INEQUALITY

Ha-Joon Chang's, *Kicking Away the Ladder*
David Graeber's, *Debt: The First 5000 Years*
Robert E. Lucas's, *Why Doesn't Capital Flow from Rich To Poor Countries?*
Thomas Piketty's, *Capital in the Twenty-First Century*
Amartya Sen's, *Inequality Re-Examined*
Mahbub Ul Haq's, *Reflections on Human Development*

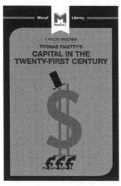

Macat analyses are available from all good bookshops and libraries.

Access hundreds of analyses through one, multimedia tool.

Join free for one month **library.macat.com**

Macat Disciplines

Access the greatest ideas and thinkers across entire disciplines, including

GLOBALIZATION

Arjun Appadurai's, *Modernity at Large: Cultural Dimensions of Globalisation*

James Ferguson's, *The Anti-Politics Machine*

Geert Hofstede's, *Culture's Consequences*

Amartya Sen's, *Development as Freedom*

Macat Disciplines

Access the greatest ideas and thinkers across entire disciplines, including

MAN AND THE ENVIRONMENT

 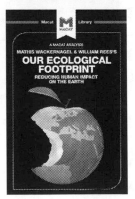

The Brundtland Report's, *Our Common Future*
Rachel Carson's, *Silent Spring*
James Lovelock's, *Gaia: A New Look at Life on Earth*
Mathis Wackernagel & William Rees's, *Our Ecological Footprint*

Macat analyses are available from all good bookshops and libraries.

Access hundreds of analyses through one, multimedia tool.
Join free for one month **library.macat.com**

Macat Disciplines

Access the greatest ideas and thinkers across entire disciplines, including

THE FUTURE OF DEMOCRACY

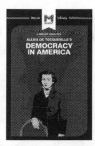

Robert A. Dahl's, *Democracy and Its Critics*
Robert A. Dahl's, *Who Governs?*
Alexis De Toqueville's, *Democracy in America*
Niccolò Machiavelli's, *The Prince*
John Stuart Mill's, *On Liberty*
Robert D. Putnam's, *Bowling Alone*
Jean-Jacques Rousseau's, *The Social Contract*
Henry David Thoreau's, *Civil Disobedience*

Macat Disciplines

Access the greatest ideas and thinkers across entire disciplines, including

TOTALITARIANISM

Sheila Fitzpatrick's, *Everyday Stalinism*
Ian Kershaw's, *The "Hitler Myth"*
Timothy Snyder's, *Bloodlands*

Macat analyses are available from all good bookshops and libraries.

Access hundreds of analyses through one, multimedia tool.

Join free for one month **library.macat.com**

Macat Pairs

Analyse historical and modern issues from opposite sides of an argument. Pairs include:

RACE AND IDENTITY

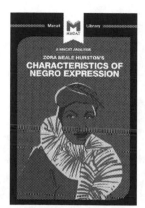

Zora Neale Hurston's
Characteristics of Negro Expression

Using material collected on anthropological expeditions to the South, Zora Neale Hurston explains how expression in African American culture in the early twentieth century departs from the art of white America. At the time, African American art was often criticized for copying white culture. For Hurston, this criticism misunderstood how art works. European tradition views art as something fixed. But Hurston describes a creative process that is alive, ever-changing, and largely improvisational. She maintains that African American art works through a process called 'mimicry'—where an imitated object or verbal pattern, for example, is reshaped and altered until it becomes something new, novel—and worthy of attention.

Frantz Fanon's
Black Skin, White Masks

Black Skin, White Masks offers a radical analysis of the psychological effects of colonization on the colonized.

Fanon witnessed the effects of colonization first hand both in his birthplace, Martinique, and again later in life when he worked as a psychiatrist in another French colony, Algeria. His text is uncompromising in form and argument. He dissects the dehumanizing effects of colonialism, arguing that it destroys the native sense of identity, forcing people to adapt to an alien set of values—including a core belief that they are inferior. This results in deep psychological trauma.

Fanon's work played a pivotal role in the civil rights movements of the 1960s.

Macat analyses are available from all good bookshops and libraries.

Access hundreds of analyses through one, multimedia tool.
Join free for one month **library.macat.com**

Macat Pairs

Analyse historical and modern issues from opposite sides of an argument. Pairs include:

INTERNATIONAL RELATIONS IN THE 21ST CENTURY

Samuel P. Huntington's
The Clash of Civilisations

In his highly influential 1996 book, Huntington offers a vision of a post-Cold War world in which conflict takes place not between competing ideologies but between cultures. The worst clash, he argues, will be between the Islamic world and the West: the West's arrogance and belief that its culture is a "gift" to the world will come into conflict with Islam's obstinacy and concern that its culture is under attack from a morally decadent "other."

Clash inspired much debate between different political schools of thought. But its greatest impact came in helping define American foreign policy in the wake of the 2001 terrorist attacks in New York and Washington.

Francis Fukuyama's
The End of History and the Last Man

Published in 1992, *The End of History and the Last Man* argues that capitalist democracy is the final destination for all societies. Fukuyama believed democracy triumphed during the Cold War because it lacks the "fundamental contradictions" inherent in communism and satisfies our yearning for freedom and equality. Democracy therefore marks the endpoint in the evolution of ideology, and so the "end of history." There will still be "events," but no fundamental change in ideology.

Macat Pairs

Analyse historical and modern issues from opposite sides of an argument. Pairs include:

HOW TO RUN AN ECONOMY

John Maynard Keynes's
The General Theory OF Employment, Interest and Money

Classical economics suggests that market economies are self-correcting in times of recession or depression, and tend toward full employment and output. But English economist John Maynard Keynes disagrees.

In his ground-breaking 1936 study *The General Theory*, Keynes argues that traditional economics has misunderstood the causes of unemployment. Employment is not determined by the price of labor; it is directly linked to demand. Keynes believes market economies are by nature unstable, and so require government intervention. Spurred on by the social catastrophe of the Great Depression of the 1930s, he sets out to revolutionize the way the world thinks

Milton Friedman's
The Role of Monetary Policy

Friedman's 1968 paper changed the course of economic theory. In just 17 pages, he demolished existing theory and outlined an effective alternate monetary policy designed to secure 'high employment, stable prices and rapid growth.'

Friedman demonstrated that monetary policy plays a vital role in broader economic stability and argued that economists got their monetary policy wrong in the 1950s and 1960s by misunderstanding the relationship between inflation and unemployment. Previous generations of economists had believed that governments could permanently decrease unemployment by permitting inflation—and vice versa. Friedman's most original contribution was to show that this supposed trade-off is an illusion that only works in the short term.

Macat analyses are available from all good bookshops and libraries.

Access hundreds of analyses through one, multimedia tool.
Join free for one month **library.macat.com**

Macat Pairs

*Analyse historical and modern issues
from opposite sides of an argument.
Pairs include:*

ARE WE FUNDAMENTALLY GOOD - OR BAD?

Steven Pinker's
The Better Angels of Our Nature

Stephen Pinker's gloriously optimistic 2011 book argues that, despite humanity's biological tendency toward violence, we are, in fact, less violent today than ever before. To prove his case, Pinker lays out pages of detailed statistical evidence. For him, much of the credit for the decline goes to the eighteenth-century Enlightenment movement, whose ideas of liberty, tolerance, and respect for the value of human life filtered down through society and affected how people thought. That psychological change led to behavioral change—and overall we became more peaceful. Critics countered that humanity could never overcome the biological urge toward violence; others argued that Pinker's statistics were flawed.

Philip Zimbardo's
The Lucifer Effect

Some psychologists believe those who commit cruelty are innately evil. Zimbardo disagrees. In *The Lucifer Effect*, he argues that sometimes good people do evil things simply because of the situations they find themselves in, citing many historical examples to illustrate his point. Zimbardo details his 1971 Stanford prison experiment, where ordinary volunteers playing guards in a mock prison rapidly became abusive. But he also describes the tortures committed by US army personnel in Iraq's Abu Ghraib prison in 2003—and how he himself testified in defence of one of those guards. committed by US army personnel in Iraq's Abu Ghraib prison in 2003—and how he himself testified in defence of one of those guards.

Macat analyses are available from all good bookshops and libraries.

Access hundreds of analyses through one, multimedia tool.

Join free for one month **library.macat.com**

Macat Pairs

*Analyse historical and modern issues
from opposite sides of an argument.
Pairs include:*

HOW WE RELATE TO EACH OTHER AND SOCIETY

Jean-Jacques Rousseau's
The Social Contract

Rousseau's famous work sets out the radical concept of the 'social contract': a give-and-take relationship between individual freedom and social order.

If people are free to do as they like, governed only by their own sense of justice, they are also vulnerable to chaos and violence. To avoid this, Rousseau proposes, they should agree to give up some freedom to benefit from the protection of social and political organization. But this deal is only just if societies are led by the collective needs and desires of the people, and able to control the private interests of individuals. For Rousseau, the only legitimate form of government is rule by the people.

Robert D. Putnam's
Bowling Alone

In *Bowling Alone*, Robert Putnam argues that Americans have become disconnected from one another and from the institutions of their common life, and investigates the consequences of this change.

Looking at a range of indicators, from membership in formal organizations to the number of invitations being extended to informal dinner parties, Putnam demonstrates that Americans are interacting less and creating less "social capital" – with potentially disastrous implications for their society.

It would be difficult to overstate the impact of *Bowling Alone*, one of the most frequently cited social science publications of the last half-century.

Printed in the United States
by Baker & Taylor Publisher Services